CREATING
WOODEN
BOXES
on the Scroll Saw

CREATING
WOODEN
BOXES
on the Scroll Saw

**Patterns and Instructions for
Jewelry, Music, and Other
Keepsake Boxes**

From the editors of
Scroll Saw Woodworking & Crafts

**Fantasy Keepsake Box
By Sue Chrestensen
Based on designs
by Lora S. Irish, page 54**

FOX CHAPEL
PUBLISHING

© 2009 by Fox Chapel Publishing Company, Inc., East Petersburg, PA.

Creating Wooden Boxes on the Scroll Saw is an original work, first published in 2009 by Fox Chapel Publishing Company, Inc. The patterns contained herein are copyrighted by the authors. Readers may make copies of these patterns for personal use. The patterns themselves, however, are not to be duplicated for resale or distribution under any circumstances. Any such copying is a violation of copyright law.

ISBN 978-1-56523-444-4

Library of Congress Cataloging-in-Publication Data

Creating wooden boxes on the scroll saw / by the editors of Scroll saw woodworking & crafts.

   p. cm. -- (The best of Scroll saw woodworking & crafts magazine)

Includes index.

ISBN: 978-1-56523-444-4

1. Woodwork. 2. Wooden boxes. 3. Jig saws. I. Scroll saw woodworking & crafts.

TT200.C84 2009
684'.08--dc22

2009019687

To learn more about the other great books from Fox Chapel Publishing, or to find a retailer near you, call toll-free 800-457-9112 or visit us at *www.FoxChapelPublishing.com*.

Note to Authors: We are always looking for talented authors to write new books. Please send a brief letter describing your idea to Acquisition Editor, 1970 Broad Street, East Petersburg, PA 17520.

Printed in China
Third printing

Table of Contents

What You Can Make

Functional Boxes

Potpourri Box
Page 19

Holiday Card Holder
Page 43

Texas Hold-'Em Caddie
Page 74

Nesting Basket Trio
Page 77

Maple Leaf Jewelry Box
Page 83

Patriotic Flag Box
Page 94

Mirrored Flower Box with
Copper and Patina Page 114

Magazine Storage Case
Page 118

Fantasy Boxes

Swan Lake Keepsake Box
Page 14

Fantasy Keepsake Boxes
Page 54

Fantasy Keepsake Boxes
Page 54

Dragon Chest
Page 63

Keepsake and Jewelry Boxes

Walnut and Brass Keepsake Box Page 38

Petal-Perfect Rose Box Page 48

Eagle Keepsake Box Page 52

Hanging Backpack Box Page 60

Four-in-One Boxes Page 89

Slope-Sided Box Page 110

Ribbons and Bows Box Page 121

Antique-Inspired Boxes

Gentleman's Box Page 22

Renaissance Keepsake Box Page 26

Victorian Fretwork Music Box Page 30

Good Luck Box Page 35

Puzzle Boxes

Sliding Panel Puzzle Box Page 100

Secret Chamber Puzzle Box Page 106

Introduction

Scroll Saw Woodworking & Crafts magazine presents a collection of the best box patterns for scroll sawers. On the following pages, you'll find patterns, tips, techniques, and stories from many of our contributors, hopefully along with inspiration to try the boxes shown in the book and your own variations and new creations.

The boxes contained here are broken down into categories—Fretwork Boxes, Segmentation and Intarsia Boxes, Layered Boxes, and One-of-a-Kind Boxes—to help you find just what you're looking for.

Hanging Backpack Box,
by Sue Chrestensen, page 60

Scroll Sawing Basics

If you're new to scrolling, read through the following information before you actually begin at your saw.

Safety. Though the scroll saw is a relatively safe tool, take the time to make sure you're working safely. Check that your work area is clean, well lit, well ventilated, and uncluttered. A dust collector, mask, air cleaner, or a combination of these items can help protect your lungs from fine dust. Wear some type of safety goggles just in case a piece of wood should break free and fly toward your face and eyes. Remove any loose clothing or jewelry before you operate the saw. Don't work while you are tired, and, of course, keep your hands and fingers a safe distance away from the blade.

Tools. Gather your tools before you begin so everything is close at hand. The projects here list the general tools you'll need and often give other suggestions and options. Remember, the lists are simply guidelines and you should always work with tools you feel comfortable using.

Squaring the blade. Before you begin any cutting, always check that your blade is square, or 90° to the scroll saw table. This will ensure your cuts are accurate. You can use any type of square to check the angle of the blade to the table. If you don't have a square, try the kerf-test method using a piece of scrap wood. First, make a small cut, about 1⁄16" long, in a piece of scrap wood about 1¾" thick. Stop the saw. Then, turn the scrap wood around until the cut is facing the back of the blade. Slide the wood across the table so that the blade fits into the cut. If the blade slips easily into the cut, it is square. If the blade does not slip easily into the cut, adjust the table and perform the test again until the blade slips in easily and is square.

Stack cutting. This technique of simply adhering together and cutting more than one piece of wood at the same time can save you time and effort. It can also ensure a better fit for identical pieces. Pieces of wood can be held together with double-sided tape, painter's or masking tape around the edges, or nails tacked into the waste areas of the wood. If you use nails, be careful that the ends of the nails do not poke through too much and scratch your saw table. If they do poke through, you can use a hammer or sandpaper to make them flush with the bottom of the stack.

Familiarize yourself with the project. It's always a good idea to read through the instructions before you begin to make sure that you understand everything that's involved.

Tools and Supplies

Scroll saw and blades of choice.

Clamps.

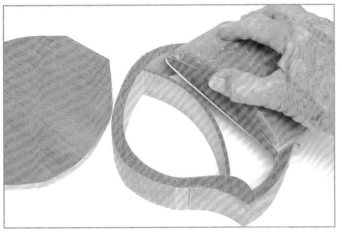

Sandpaper.

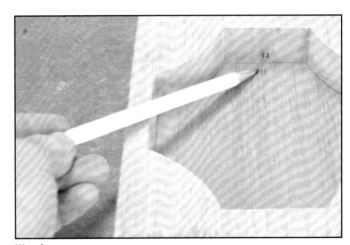

Wood.

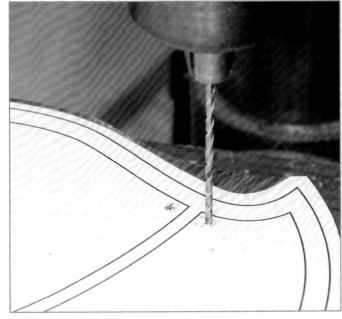

Drill and bits.

Finish of choice.

Fretwork Boxes

Fretwork projects, boxes included, are often characterized by their large amounts of inside cuts and their sometimes delicate and difficult look. These boxes range from simple to more challenging, and they can be both functional and decorative.

Gentleman's Box,
by John A. Nelson, page 22.

Swan Lake Keepsake Box

Elegance and grace are always in style

By Diana Thompson

TIP **CLAMPING HINT**

Clamping spare blocks to the work piece helps hold it steady and level while cutting. Attach the clamps only tight enough to hold the work and not so tight that the blade cannot move through the kerf.

I often find creative inspiration in common items we see every day but take for granted. I was doodling with a drawing program on my computer when I realized I could make boxes in a variety of styles and sizes. Boxes are fun to make. They are also great gifts with that handmade, personal touch.

Carefully consider the type of wood you want to use. New scrollers may want to try basswood, white pine, sugar pine, or any kind of cedar. Remember, the softer the wood, the easier it is to cut. I made the box you see in the photo from genuine mahogany.

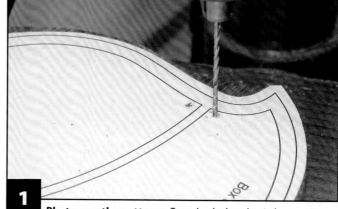

1 **Photocopy the patterns.** To make the box, begin by spraying the pattern for the box sides with temporary bond spray adhesive. Attach it to the ¾" to 1¼" stock. Use a drill with a ¹⁄₁₆"-diameter bit to make blade entry holes in each opening. A larger bit, such as one with a ³⁄₃₂" diameter, can also be used.

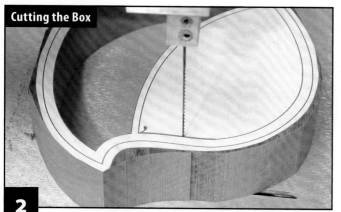

Cutting the Box

2 **Cut the inside line.** Thread the #7 blade through the entry holes and begin cutting. Cut only the inside line, leaving the outside line to be cut later. Do not remove the pattern.

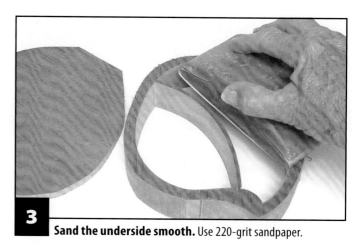

3 **Sand the underside smooth.** Use 220-grit sandpaper.

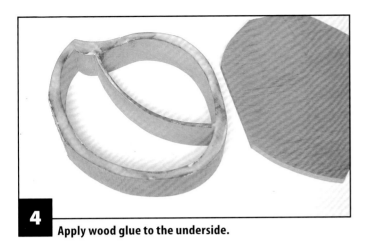

4 Apply wood glue to the underside.

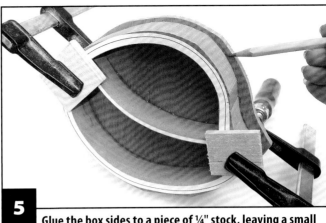

5 **Glue the box sides to a piece of ¼" stock, leaving a small margin around the edge.** Approximately six clamps are needed. Only two are shown here for clarity. Allow the glue to dry at least an hour.

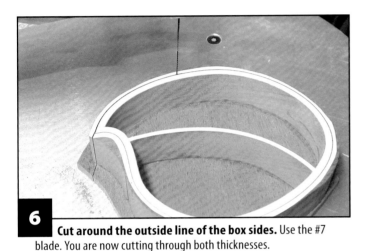

6 **Cut around the outside line of the box sides.** Use the #7 blade. You are now cutting through both thicknesses.

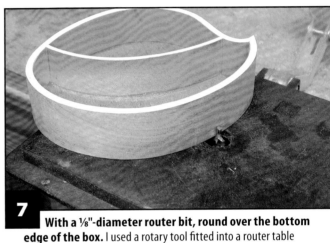

7 **With a ⅛"-diameter router bit, round over the bottom edge of the box.** I used a rotary tool fitted into a router table attachment. This step can also be done by hand with sandpaper.

Making the Lid

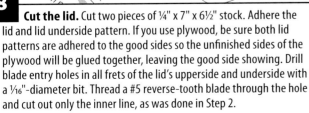

8 **Cut the lid.** Cut two pieces of ¼" x 7" x 6½" stock. Adhere the lid and lid underside pattern. If you use plywood, be sure both lid patterns are adhered to the good sides so the unfinished sides of the plywood will be glued together, leaving the good side showing. Drill blade entry holes in all frets of the lid's upperside and underside with a ¹⁄₁₆"-diameter bit. Thread a #5 reverse-tooth blade through the hole and cut out only the inner line, as was done in Step 2.

9 **Lid and lid underside are cut and ready to glue together.**

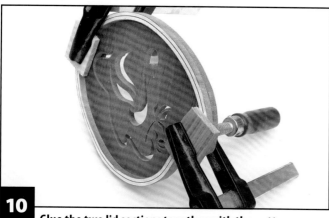

10 **Glue the two lid sections together with the pattern sides facing out.** Clamp the two sections into place as in Step 5 and allow them to dry for at least an hour. About six clamps are needed. Only two are shown for clarity.

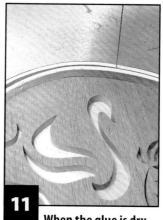

11 When the glue is dry, cut around the centerline of the lid underside as in **Step 6.** You're cutting through both thicknesses.

12 Round over the upper and lower edges of the lid as in Step 7.

Cutting the Handle

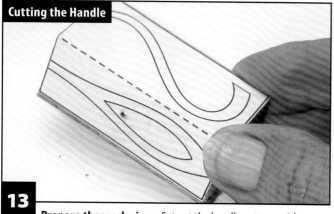

13 **Prepare the work piece.** Cut out the handle pattern with scissors and fold it along the dashed line. Apply temporary bond spray adhesive to the back of the pattern and wrap it around two sides of the ¾" x 1" x 2" wood. Drill a blade entry hole in the left side using a ⅟₁₆"-diameter bit.

14 **Cut the handle.** Thread the #5 blade through the entry hole. Cut the inside fret first, leaving it in place. Then cut the outside lines.

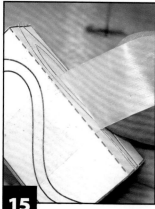

15 **Tape the block.** Allowing the figure to rest naturally in the block, gently pinch the sides together and tape around it with ¾" cellophane tape.

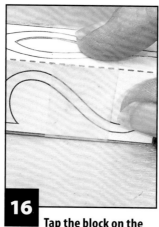

16 Tap the block on the saw table to ensure the figure is flush inside the block.

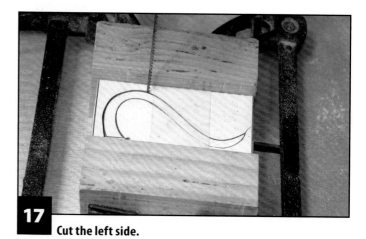

17 Cut the left side.

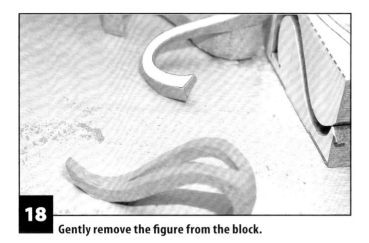

18 Gently remove the figure from the block.

19 **Finish the box.** Apply a wood sealer to all pieces. I prefer a water-based sealer due to the easy cleanup. However, it will raise the grain a bit, so after the sealer is dry, sand the box smooth with 220-grit sandpaper and finish with #00000 steel wool. Glue the handle to the box lid. Apply several coats of clear finish. I use Krylon spray because it doesn't discolor over time.

Lid Underside

Handle

Photocopy at 100%

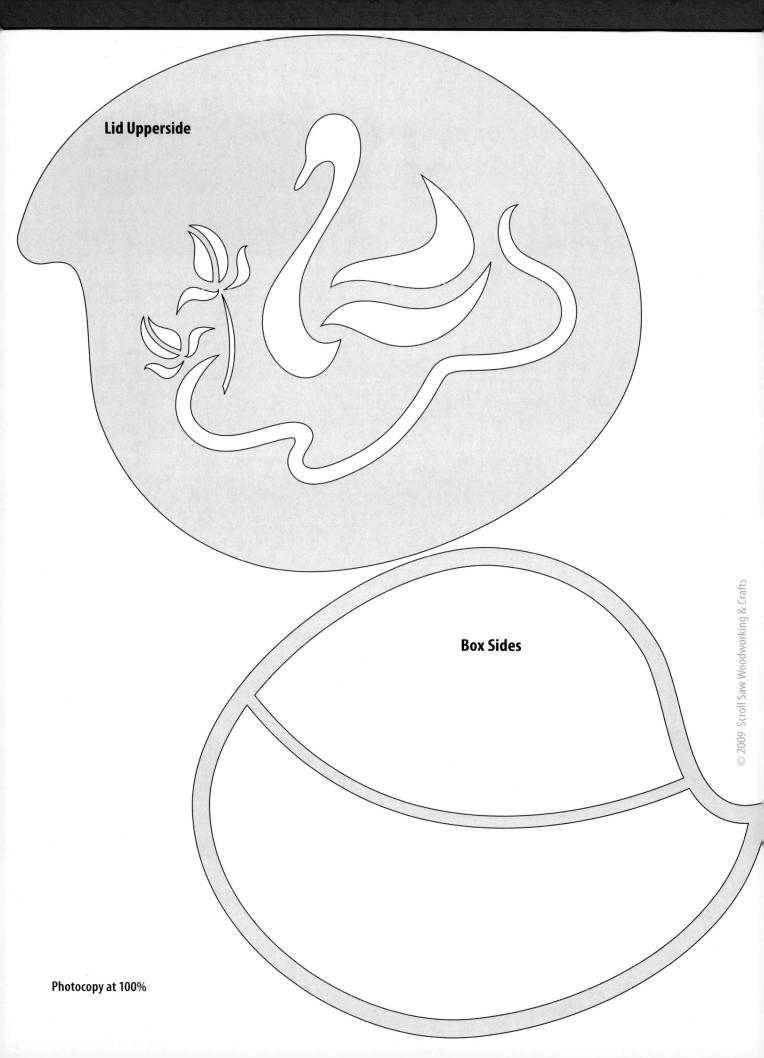

Lid Upperside

Box Sides

Photocopy at 100%

Potpourri Box

Scroll this box to hold aromatic potpourri or watch a candle flame dance through the scrolled-out images. Never use the lid or leave unattended when burning a candle in the holder.

This attractive potpourri box quickly converts to a tea light candleholder.

By Sue Mey

Nothing makes a place smell more like home than potpourri, but it tends to get everywhere—especially if you have furry friends. To keep the dried flowers and herbs where they belong, use a potpourri box.

This potpourri box with lid was inspired by celestial bodies. I stack cut the pattern and made one in hardwood and another in medium density fiberboard (MDF), which I painted. The item can also be used as an attractive tea light or flat candleholder without the lid. Do not place the holder in a draft, which could bring the flame into contact with the wood. Constant supervision is advised.

Step 1: Sand all hardwood pieces. Use a palm sander with 320 grit to sand both sides. This reduces the hand sanding after cutting. MDF does not require pre-sanding.

Step 2: Attach the patterns to the wood. Photocopy the pattern pieces at 100% and attach them to the wood using temporary bond spray adhesive. Or, for simple patterns such as these, I like to transfer the pattern to the work piece with carbon paper and a stylus. Keep the pattern in place with two small pieces of masking tape.

Step 3: Tape two or more blanks together to stack cut the box. To create multiple boxes at once, attach extra layers of wood or MDF to the piece with the pattern on it. Use small strips of thin double-sided tape at the corners to hold the layers together. **Note:** The lid liner can not be stack cut because it will be attached to the lid before the pierce cuts are made. They can, however, be stacked for the disc sander process (see Step 8), before you attach a separate pattern to each lid liner.

Step 4: Drill the blade entry holes. Use the 3/32"-diameter bit for the box sides and the 1/16"-diameter bit for the features of the sun pattern. **Note:** Do not drill the lid liner blade entry holes at this time.

Step 5: Remove the burrs created by drilling the holes. Use a scraper blade at a slight angle along the grain of the wood.

TIP **A BIT OF GOLD**

If you decide to make the painted MDF box, splatter a little bit of gold paint on the box to add texture. Working fast, spray some gold paint onto paper, dip an old toothbrush into the paint, and run a plastic ruler over the brush. Vary the direction of the spray onto the box to avoid uniform splashes. Or, if you don't mind getting paint on your fingers, dip your middle finger in the paint and flick the paint randomly on the box.

▲ Step 6: Make the inside cuts on the four box sides. Thread the #5 blade through the blade entry holes and make the inside cuts of the box sides—you can stack cut two layers at the same time. Use a #3 blade for the sun's features. **Note:** Do not cut the lid liner at this time.

▲ Step 7: Cut the scalloped edge of the lid and base. To do this neatly, cut into the sharp point from the edge. Back out of the cut, and then cut into the sharp point from the other direction.

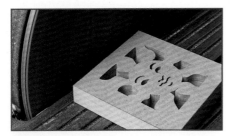

▲ Step 8: Square the edges of the sides and lid liner on the disc sander. For this project, edges should line up nicely, and I find using the disc sander much easier than attempting to cut perfectly straight edges with the scroll saw.

Step 9: Separate the wood layers. Insert a scraper blade between the work pieces to pull them apart. Remove the sticky tape residue with a rag and some mineral spirits. Allow them to dry.

▲ Step 10: Apply wood glue to the back surface of the lid liner. Then, center the liner on the inside of the lid. Clamp the four corners and the center. Remove excess glue with a damp rag or toothpick. Once dry, apply/copy the pattern for the pierce cuts, if not done earlier. Drill blade entry holes and make the cuts.

Step 11: Sand the hardwood pieces by hand. Use 320 grit, after removing the patterns. Then, switch to 500 grit to get a smooth finish. Only lightly sand the cut edges of the MDF to remove any burrs.

Step 12: Glue the box. First, remove all sanding dust. Dry-fit the four box sides on the base to ensure all edges line up nicely. If needed, mark any adjustments and sand them to shape. Apply wood glue to the box sides, one at a time, and place them on the base. Hold the four box sides in position with both hands. Then, center them on the base and press down hard. Exert equal pressure on the sun and moon face sides to ensure the moon and star sides are firmly attached. Remove excess glue with a toothpick or damp rag. I do not use clamps, but you may need to use them depending on the glue you choose.

▲Step 13: Apply the finish. For the hardwood box, apply a deep penetrating furniture wax liquid with a medium-size artist's brush. The brush will reach the nooks and crannies of the pierce cuts. Place the box and lid in the sun to dry. If this is not possible, allow a day or two before varnishing. Wipe all box surfaces with a dry, lint-free cloth. You can also apply Danish oil according to manufacturer's directions.

For the MDF box, spray the inside and outside of the box and lid with several thin coats of spray paint, allowing it to dry completely between coats. Remove spray paint from fingers and utensils with lacquer thinner.

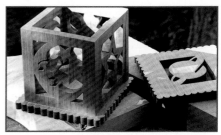

▲ Step 14: Apply the final finish. Apply several thin coats of clear spray varnish to the hardwood box, allowing it to dry thoroughly between coats. The painted box does not need to be varnished. Fill the box with your favorite mix of potpourri, replace the lid, and place it near an open window to disperse the fragrance into the room. Alternatively, light a fragrant tea light and place it inside the open box. **Note:** *Never* use the lid with a candle—and *never* leave a burning candle unattended!

TIP **WARMING UP WAX**

Pour the wax liquid into an old ceramic mug and heat it in a microwave oven for 15 seconds. This allows the wax to liquefy and penetrate the wood without leaving a waxy layer.

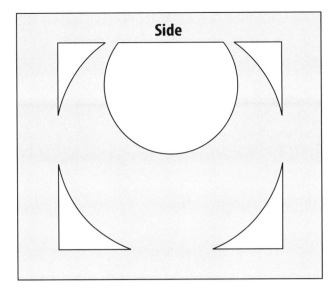

Side

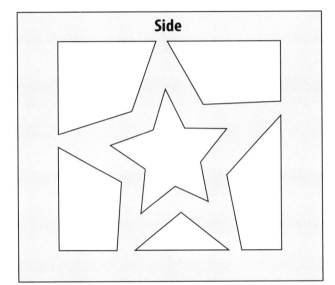

Side

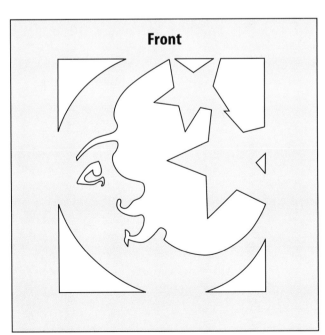

Front

Photocopy at 100%

Materials:
- ¼" x 12" x 3⁵⁄₃₂" hardwood of choice or MDF (box sides)
- ¼" x 8" x 4" hardwood of choice or MDF (base and lid)
- ⅛" x 2⅝" x 2⅝" hardwood of choice or MDF (lid liner)
- Sandpaper, assorted grits
- Temporary bond spray adhesive or carbon paper and stylus
- Thin double-sided tape
- Spray paint in color of choice (if using MDF)

Materials & Tools

- Quick-dry wood glue
- Damp rag for removal of excess glue
- Deep penetrating furniture wax liquid or Danish oil and an artist's brush
- Clear spray varnish

Tools:
- #5 reverse-tooth blade
- #3 reverse-tooth blade
- Drill press with ³⁄₃₂"- and ¹⁄₁₆"-diameter bits
- Disc sander and palm sander
- Small clamps

Back

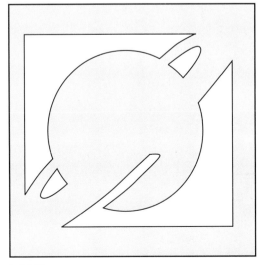

Lid and base (outer line only)

Lid liner

© 2009 Scroll Saw Woodworking & Crafts

Gentleman's Box

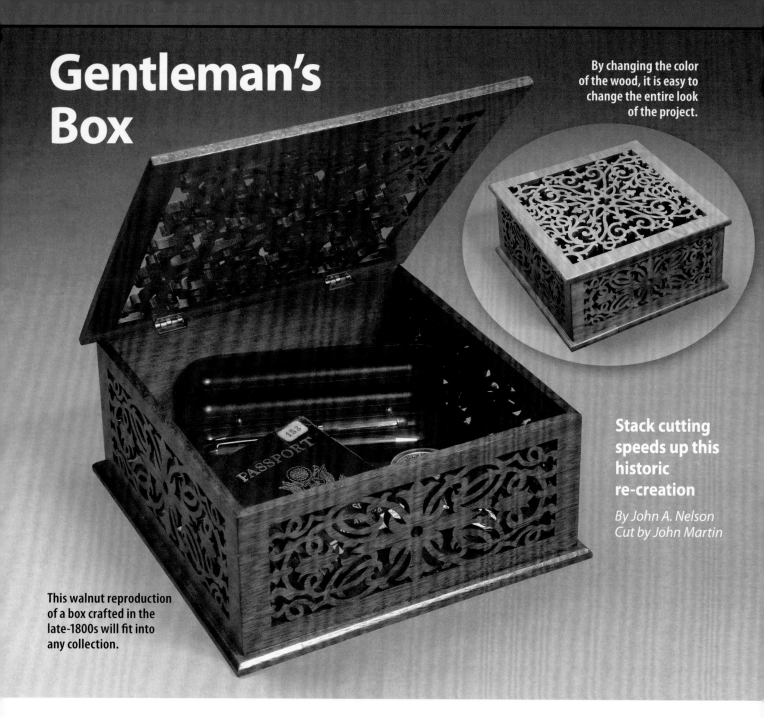

By changing the color of the wood, it is easy to change the entire look of the project.

Stack cutting speeds up this historic re-creation

By John A. Nelson
Cut by John Martin

This walnut reproduction of a box crafted in the late-1800s will fit into any collection.

I found this beautiful, simple box in an antique shop along Route 1, just south of Kennebunkport, Maine. The original was made of walnut. A silk lining was first glued to a cardboard backing before both were glued into the box.

Step 1: Choose wood with an interesting grain pattern. I suggest walnut, maple, or black cherry. If needed, glue up material to make the lid and the bottom. Cut all of the wood to size using the provided materials list.

Step 2: Cut a 6° bevel on all four edges of the top to knock off the sharp corners. If you are confident cutting the bevels on the scroll saw, simply tilt your table down 6°. Alternatively, you can sand the bevel using your sander of choice. These bevels are just embellishments that appeared on the original—you can make a box without the bevels if you want.

Step 3: Sand all the surfaces of the top. Be careful not to round over any edges.

Step 4: Cut the bottom to the exact size. Put a 30° bevel on all four edges. Use the techniques explained in Step 2. Again, sand all of the surfaces of the bottom, but be careful not to round over any edges.

Step 5: Cut all four sides to size. Cut an exact 45° bevel for the miter joints on the sides of each piece. If you don't have a table saw to cut the miters, use a disk sander with a miter gauge. Set the miter gauge to 45° and slowly sand the edge down to the proper miter. You can cut the miters with a scroll saw, but it is difficult to get the miters to fit tightly.

Step 6: Use masking tape to tape the four sides together. Make sure all the joints fit together exactly (see Making Miter Joints).

Step 7: Cut a sub-base to fit tightly inside all four sides. This helps the box hold its shape. Plywood is recommended to reduce any expansion (or contraction) in one direction. The sub-base can be embellished with felt, flocking, or silk.

Step 8: Remove the tape. Then, sand the top and bottom surfaces of the sides.

Step 9: Mark and notch one side for the hinges as shown on the pattern. Re-sand that side, which will be the back of the box, to make sure it's smooth.

Step 10: Prepare the lid. Center the lid pattern on the top and attach it using temporary bond spray adhesive. Then, drill blade entry holes to make the interior cuts.

Step 11: Cut out the pattern. Use a #2 or #3 blade or your blade of choice.

Step 12: Sand the top and bottom surfaces of the lid. Use fine-grit sandpaper.

Step 13: Prepare the sides. Make three copies of the side pattern and attach them to the right side, left side, and front blanks using spray adhesive. Do not attach a pattern to the back piece, which was notched for the hinges.

Step 14: Drill blade entry holes and cut out the fretwork on each side. Alternatively, stack all three sides together, and wrap all four edges with masking tape. Then, you can stack cut all three sides at once.

Step 15: Sand all of the sides' surfaces with fine-grit sandpaper.

Step 16: Apply wood glue to the 45° miter cuts on all four sides. Using the masking tape technique explained in Step 6, assemble all four sides, and allow the glue to dry. Remove any excess glue.

Step 17: Center the four sides on the base and insert the sub-base from the top. Predrill holes from the base into the sides, and insert tiny brads for a permanent assembly.

Step 18: Apply the finish of your choice.

Step 19: Attach the lid with two brass hinges. Again, predrill the holes for the screws so you don't split the wood.

Step 20: Cut cardboard to fit the four sides and lid (optional). Add silk, felt, or your covering of choice to the sub-base of the box (optional). You can also paint the cardboard and glue it in place. The original had silk glued to the cardboard liner on the four sides and lid. Alternatively, you could add flocking according to the manufacturer's directions.

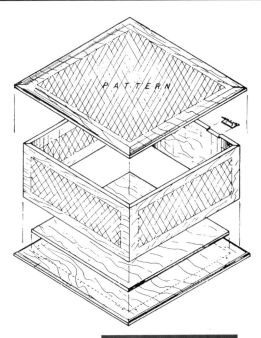

Materials & Tools

Materials:
- 2 pieces ³⁄₁₆" x 9½" x 9½" hardwood of choice (top and bottom)
- 4 pieces ³⁄₁₆" x 3⁹⁄₁₆" x 8⅞" hardwood of choice (sides)
- ³⁄₁₆" x 8½" x 8½" plywood of choice (sub-base)
- 2 brass hinges, ³⁄₁₆" x 1"
- 12 brads, ⅝" long
- Silk backing over cardboard or flocking of choice
- Wood finish of choice
- Wood glue
- Masking tape
- Repositionable spray adhesive

Tools:
- #3 blades or blades of choice
- Drill with ¹⁄₁₆"-diameter drill bit
- Assorted grits of sandpaper

MAKING MITER JOINTS

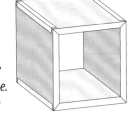

There are several ways to glue up a miter joint box.
For beginners, the easiest way is to use the tape method.
Start by cutting four lengths of tape slightly shorter than the height of the box (approximately 3"). Place the tape face up on the workbench and stick side one of the box to the tape. Align the edge of side two exactly alongside the edge of side one (see diagram) and press both sides firmly against the tape. Apply wood glue to all the joints and bring side four back around to join side one. Check to make sure the box is square using a square to check the outside corners or by inserting the sub-base into the box.

Sides

Position of hinges (back of box only)

Photocopy at 100%

Cut perimeter only for box bottom.

Photocopy at 100%

Top and bottom shown here to facilitate placement.

Renaissance Keepsake Box

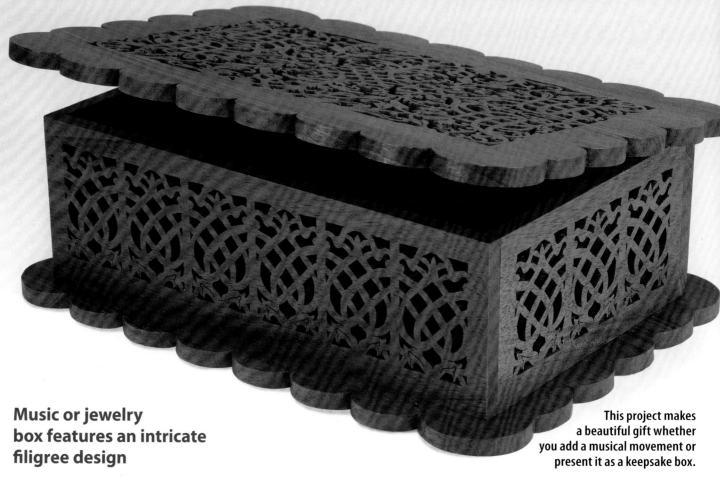

Music or jewelry box features an intricate filigree design

By Rick and Karen Longabaugh
Cut by Ben Fink

This project makes a beautiful gift whether you add a musical movement or present it as a keepsake box.

Handmade gifts make a lasting impression. This vintage-inspired keepsake box is sure to impress even the most discerning recipient. Choose a musical movement that plays a tune with a special meaning or leave the bottom solid so the intended recipient can use it as a trinket or jewelry box.

This box is made from Honduras-mahogany, but a variety of woods are suitable. Cut the pieces to the proper dimensions. Cut the fretwork design in the lid before cutting the perimeter. Stack the top and bottom together to cut the scalloped borders at the same time. If you make small errors while cutting the perimeter, the two pieces will be identical, and the mistakes will be less noticeable. Stack cut the long and short sides to speed production time

If you are installing a musical movement, drill the ⅜"-diameter hole for the music box key where indicated on the pattern. If presenting the box without the musical movement, the feet to raise the box are optional. Cut the feet using standard compound-cutting techniques.

After cutting all of the pieces, glue all four sides to the bottom using the dotted lines on the pattern as a guide. Tabs on the long box sides make alignment easier. Glue the feet to the bottom of the box. Apply your finish of choice to the assembled box and the lid. Then, install the music box mechanism and attach the lid to the box using small brass hinges. Use thin plywood or cardboard wrapped in felt for an optional lining behind the fretwork sides and lid.

Lid
Stock: ¼"

Use hinges of your choice to attach the lid to the back.

Photocopy at 100%

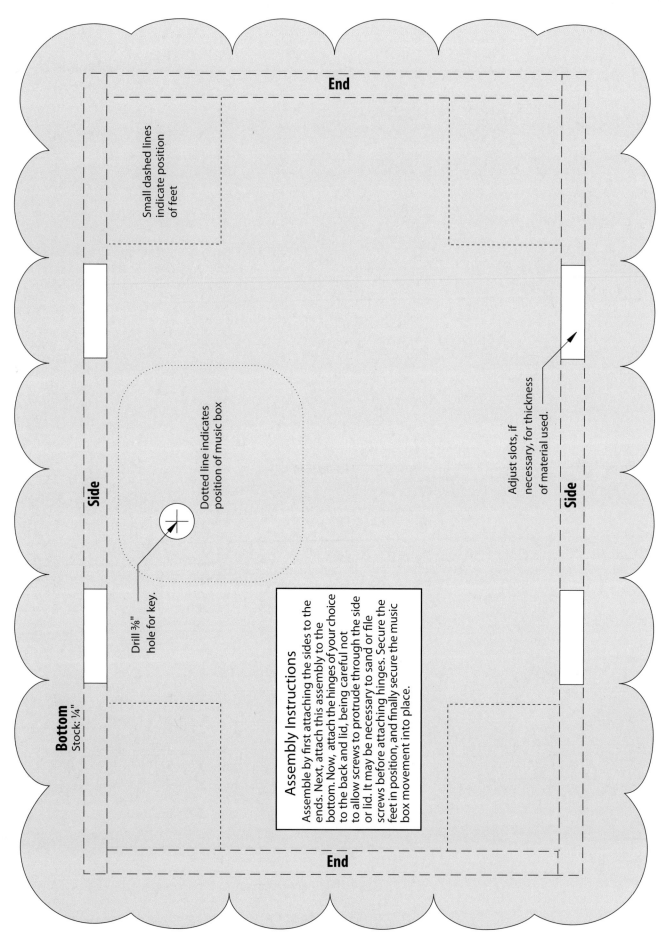

End

Small dashed lines indicate position of feet

Side

Dotted line indicates position of music box

Drill ⅜" hole for key.

Adjust slots, if necessary, for thickness of material used.

Side

Bottom
Stock: ¼"

Assembly Instructions

Assemble by first attaching the sides to the ends. Next, attach this assembly to the bottom. Now, attach the hinges of your choice to the back and lid, being careful not to allow screws to protrude through the side or lid. It may be necessary to sand or file screws before attaching hinges. Secure the feet in position, and finally secure the music box movement into place.

End

Photocopy at 100%

Use hinges of your choice to attach the Lid to the back Side.

Side
Stock: ¼", cut 2

Attach ends with glue and finishing nails.

End
Stock: ¼", cut 2

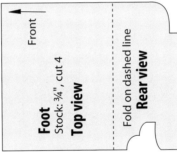

Front

Foot
Stock: ¾", cut 4
Top view

Fold on dashed line
Rear view

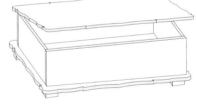

Materials & Tools

Materials:

- 2 pieces ¼" x 7¼" x 10" wood of choice (lid and bottom)
- 2 pieces ¼" x 3" x 8½" wood of choice (sides)
- 2 pieces ¼" x 2⁹⁄₁₆" x 4⁷⁄₈" wood of choice (ends)
- 4 pieces ¾" x 1¹³⁄₁₆" x 1⁹⁄₁₆" wood of choice (feet)
- Music box mechanism (optional)
- Small brass hinges with matching screws
- Assorted grits of sandpaper
- Temporary bond spray adhesive
- Wood glue

- Brads (optional, to hold sides together when glued)
- Finish of choice
- Felt (optional)

Tools:

- #1 reverse-tooth blades or blades of choice
- Drill with ¹⁄₁₆"- and ¼"-diameter drill bits
- Screwdriver to install small brass screws
- Hammer (optional)
- Brushes to apply finish of choice (optional)

Victorian Fretwork Music Box

Classic details provide an impressive look, but this vintage box is surprisingly easy to scroll

By Rick and Karen Longabaugh

This handcrafted music box is sure to become a cherished family heirloom. Even without the musical movement, the project makes a beautiful keepsake box. Try experimenting with different options—line the inside with silk or try a backing board with flocking; scroll just the top and leave the sides solid. You could even alter the pattern on the lid to include a monogram or special symbol. Customizing the box makes it a one-of-a-kind gift that is sure to please.

Step 1: Prepare your blanks. Cut all of the pieces to the dimensions listed in the materials list. Sand all of the pieces with progressively finer grits of sandpaper up to 220 grit.

Step 2: Prepare the side pieces for stack cutting. Stack the two blanks for the long sides and the two blanks for the short sides. Attach the blanks together to stack cut, using your method of choice (painter's tape, hot glue, double-sided tape, etc.).

Step 3: Transfer the patterns to the top, bottom, and side stacks. Use your method of choice (temporary bond spray adhesive, carbon paper, or graphite paper). Fold the patterns for the feet along the dotted line, and attach them to the blanks using temporary bond spray adhesive.

Step 4: Drill blade entry holes for the interior cuts on the top, sides, and bottom. Use the smallest drill bit that a #1 blade, or your blade of choice, will fit through. Drill the ⅜"-diameter hole in the bottom for the music box key. Mark and drill the pilot holes for your hinge screws at this time as well.

Step 5: Make the interior cuts on the sides and top. Start in the center with the #1 reverse-tooth blade and work your way out. Cut the slots on the bottom for the side tabs. Try to keep these slots as square as possible so the side tabs fit in tightly.

Step 6: Cut out the perimeter of the top, bottom, and sides. Use a #5 reverse-tooth blade. It is possible to stack the top and bottom together, using double-sided tape or hot glue. This way, the scalloping around the edges will be exactly the same.

Step 7: Cut out the box's feet. You only need to cut out the rear view on the scroll saw since the top view is the exact dimensions listed in the materials list. Use a #5 skip-tooth blade. The piece is very thick (1¼"-thick), so use caution, and let the saw cut at its own speed. If you try to cut too fast, the saw blade will bend, and you will get an angled cut.

Step 8: Sand the pieces with 220-grit sandpaper to remove any burrs. Apply your finish of choice. A good choice would be to dunk the pieces in Danish oil or boiled linseed oil. Dunk the pieces, bring them out, and suspend them so the oil will drain off.

Step 9: Assemble the box according to the assembly diagram. Run a bead of glue along the ends of the short sides, and nail the pieces together with small brads where indicated on the pattern. Glue the tabs on the long sides into the holes in the bottom. Make sure the screws for the hinges are not so long that they will penetrate through the wood of the top and side. Then, attach the hinges.

Step 10: Glue the feet in place on the bottom where indicated on the pattern. Use your wood glue of choice, and clamp the pieces overnight. Attach the music box movement to the bottom where indicated on the pattern. Follow the manufacturer's directions to install the music box movement.

Materials &Tools

Materials:
- 2 pieces ¼" x 8" x 10½" wood of choice (top and bottom)
- 2 pieces ¼" x 2½" x 9⅜" wood of choice (sides)
- 2 pieces ¼" x 2¼" x 5¾" wood of choice (ends)
- 4 pieces ¾" x 1¼" x 2" wood of choice (feet)
- 2 hinges, ¼" x ¾" with corresponding screws
- 8 small brads to tack sides together
- Sandpaper, assorted grits up to 220 grit
- Wood glue of choice
- Finish of choice
- Music box movement of choice

Tools:
- #1 and #5 reverse-tooth blades or blades of choice
- #5 skip-tooth blades or blades of choice
- Drill
- Assorted small-diameter drill bits
- ⅜"-diameter drill bit
- Hammer to nail in brads
- Clamps of choice

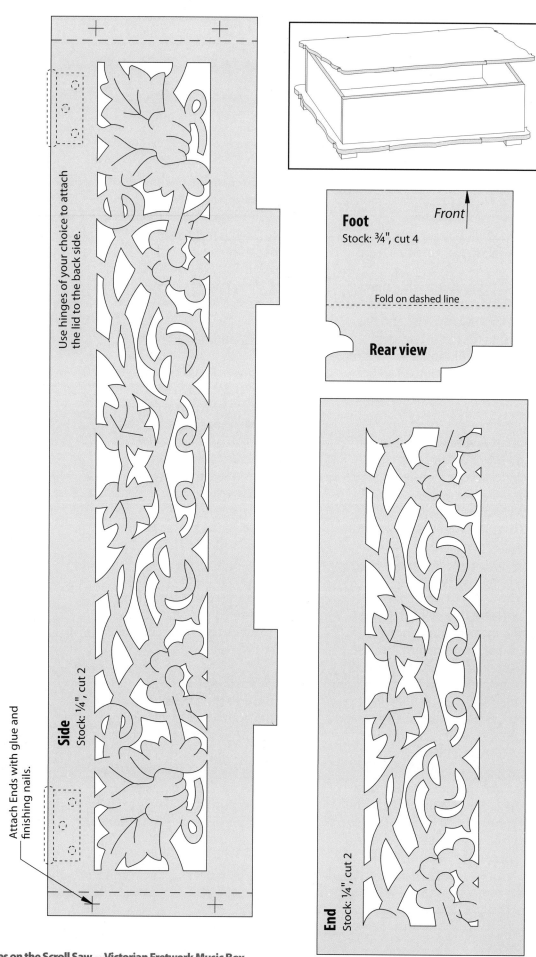

Use hinges of your choice to attach the lid to the back side.

Side
Stock: ¼", cut 2

Attach Ends with glue and finishing nails.

Foot
Stock: ¾", cut 4

Front

Fold on dashed line

Rear view

End
Stock: ¼", cut 2

Photocopy at 100%

End

Use hinges of your choice to attach the lid to the back side.

Side

Lid

Stock: ¼"

Side

End

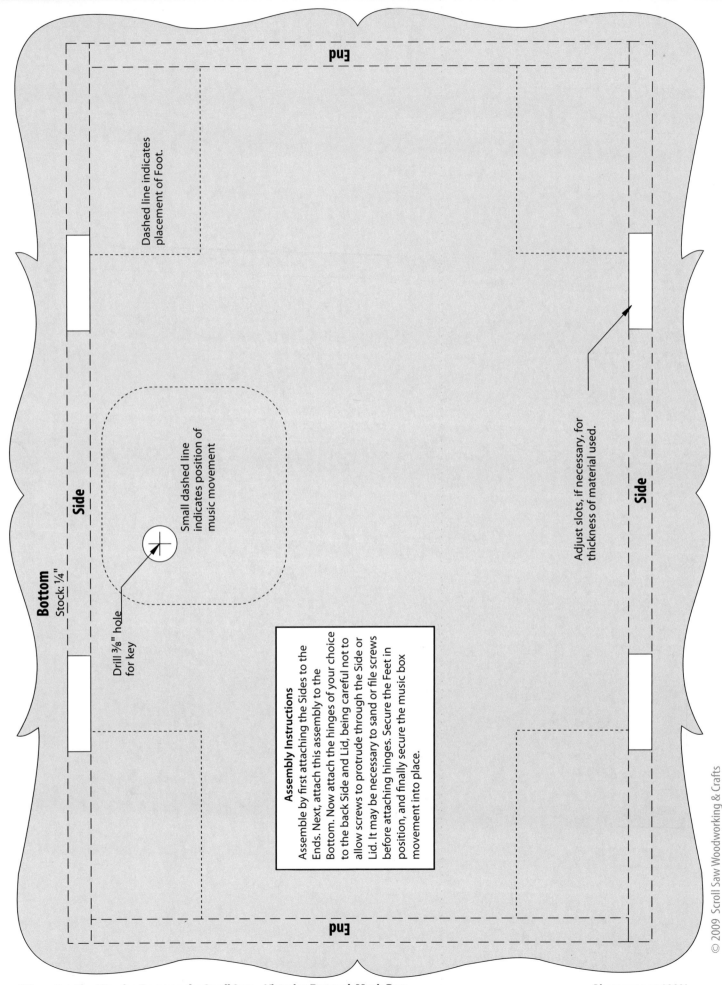

End

Dashed line indicates placement of Foot.

Side

Small dashed line indicates position of music movement

Bottom
Stock: ¼"

Drill ⅜" hole for key

Assembly Instructions

Assemble by first attaching the Sides to the Ends. Next, attach this assembly to the Bottom. Now attach the hinges of your choice to the back Side and Lid, being careful not to allow screws to protrude through the Side or Lid. It may be necessary to sand or file screws before attaching hinges. Secure the Feet in position, and finally secure the music box movement into place.

Adjust slots, if necessary, for thickness of material used.

Side

End

Good Luck Box

Recreate a classic design patterned after a Victorian box

By Joe Preston

Scroll this Victorian-influenced fretwork design as a great gift.

The idea for this project came from a box my son picked up at an antique store. They called it a Victorian document box. The top was hinged and the wear and tear from opening the box had cracked the back where the hinges were fastened. That is why I opted to make the top completely removable. I believe the original box was cut out of mahogany, but there were so many coats of finish on it, I'm not sure.

The original box was not lined, but I added a flocked interior. I did change the dimensions of the original box a little, but kept the spirit alive.

I used Baltic birch to make my box, but it looks good in black walnut with red flocking and black cherry with brown flocking. See what other combinations you can create.

Step 1: Cut all the wood to size. A table saw works best to give you straight sides and sharp corners.

Step 2: Cut the box joints. You can cut the joints on the table saw, with a router, or on the scroll saw. If cutting joints with the scroll saw, apply the pattern to corresponding pieces now; it is best to cut a little proud of the line on a scroll saw and adjust the fit by sanding. I used a scroll saw on the prototype and would highly recommend using a table saw or router. They make a much better joint.

Step 3: Cut the scalloping on the top and bottom pieces. Nail both pieces together in each corner for stack cutting. Attach the pattern to the top piece using temporary bond spray adhesive. Using the #7 blade, cut the scalloped outline on both so they will be uniform when finished. Take your time—the wood you

are cutting is both thick and hard. Designate one as the bottom and the other as the top.

Step 4: Prepare to cut the fretwork sides. Start by attaching the patterns to the wood with the spray adhesive. Then, drill blade entry holes for the fretwork on each panel.

Step 5: Cut out the fretwork on the top and sides. Start in the center and work your way outward on each piece. I cut it all using a #5 blade, but some people may prefer finer blades for the more fragile fretwork.

Step 6: Finish sand the pieces using fine sandpaper. If using a power sander, curl the edges of the paper up so they do not catch on the edges of the fragile fretwork.

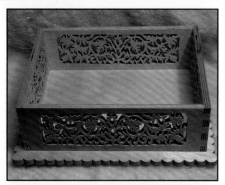

▲ **Step 7: Glue up the box sides.** Make sure the joints are sanded flush. Then, apply glue to the joints, clamp, and allow them to dry.

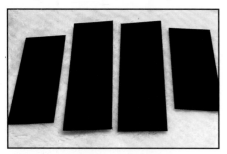

▲ **Step 8: Spray the top keeper and inside panels of the box.** Use flat black paint on one side only. Allow them to dry.

▲ **Step 9: Glue the inside panels onto the box.** The color should show through the fretwork.

▲ **Step 10: Glue the keeper to the top.** The color should again show through the fretwork. Allow everything to dry.

Step 11: Spray everything with several coats of a clear finish of your choice. Be sure to spray the inside to seal it before adding the flocking. Allow it to dry.

▲ **Step 12: Apply tape.** Tape around the edges of the box and along the edges of the keeper to contain the flocking.

Photocopy at 160%

▲ **Step 13: Apply the undercoat adhesive for flocking.** Then, apply flocking. Do the top first. Then, move on to the box interior. Allow the box to dry for 24 hours.

Step 14: Remove the masking tape and replace the cover.

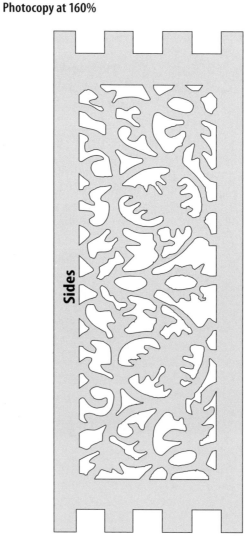

Sides

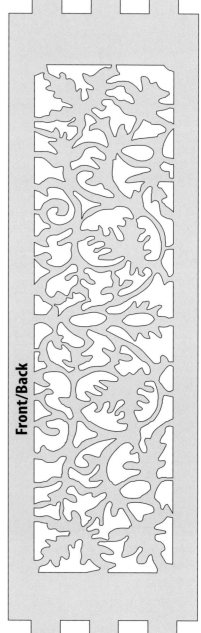

Front/Back

Lid and Bottom

Materials:

- 2 pieces ⅛" x 3" x 7⁹⁄₁₆"
  (inside sides)
- 2 pieces ⅛" x 3" x 9⅞"
  (inside front and back)
- 2 pieces ⅜" x 3¼" x 8⅜" (sides)
- 2 pieces ⅜" x 3¼" x 10⅞"
  (front and back)
- 2 pieces ⅜" x 11" x 13"
  (top & bottom)
- ⅛" x 7⁹⁄₁₆" x 10⅛" (top keeper)
- Flat black spray paint

- Clear spray finish of choice
- Black flocking kit
- Wood glue
- Masking tape or painter's tape

Tools:

- Assorted clamps (spring & bar)
- #5 blade or blade of choice for delicate fretwork
- #63 drill bit

Photocopy at 160%

Walnut and Brass Keepsake Box

Provide a safe harbor for your treasures and heirlooms with this attractive and versatile keepsake box

By Joan West

Our "collectible" memories can be as shiny as brass and as warm as walnut. This project is a chance for you to discover your scroll saw can cut more than wood. Moreover, it enables you to experience the joy of working with brass to create a lasting tribute to those personal keepsakes you hold so dear.

The soft brass plate used in this project was ordered from Showcase Brass Company Inc., but a standard door kick plate purchased from a local hardware store will work nicely. Scrap and unpolished brass are also workable if you want to invest in a can of brass polish and a little elbow grease.

I designed and sized the initials specifically for this project to compliment the unique, decorative nature of the brass pattern. Please feel free to use similar monogram styles of your choosing or whatever ornamental stencils or computer fonts that strike your fancy.

Materials:
- 9/16" x 12" x 10" walnut (base, layer 1)
- 1 1/16" x 11" x 9" walnut (box wall, layer 2)
- 1/4" x 11" x 9" walnut (lid lip, layer 3)
- 3/8" x 12" x 10" walnut (main lid, layer 4)
- 1/4" x 11" x 9" walnut (top lid, layer 6)
- 1/8" or 1/4" x 8 7/8" x 6 1/8" scrap wood
- 8 7/8" x 6 1/8" x approximately 50 mills brass (layer 5)

Tools:
- Danish oil
- Wood glue
- Clear packaging tape

Materials & Tools

- #7 blades for metal
- #7 precision ground tooth wood blades
- 1/16"-diameter drill bit
- Small chisel
- 1/4"-radius round-over router bit
- Silicon spray lubricant
- Caulk
- Temporary bond spray adhesive
- 600-grit sandpaper (for brass)
- 100-, 150-, 220-grit sandpaper (for wood)
- Bar or C-clamps
- Metal or brass polish
- Finish sander
- Rotary polishing tool (optional)

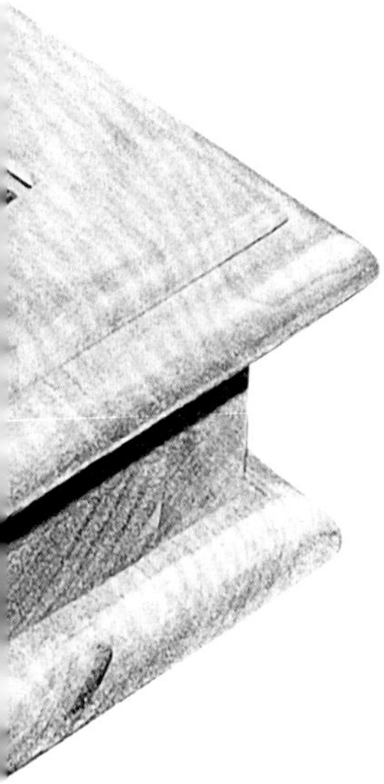

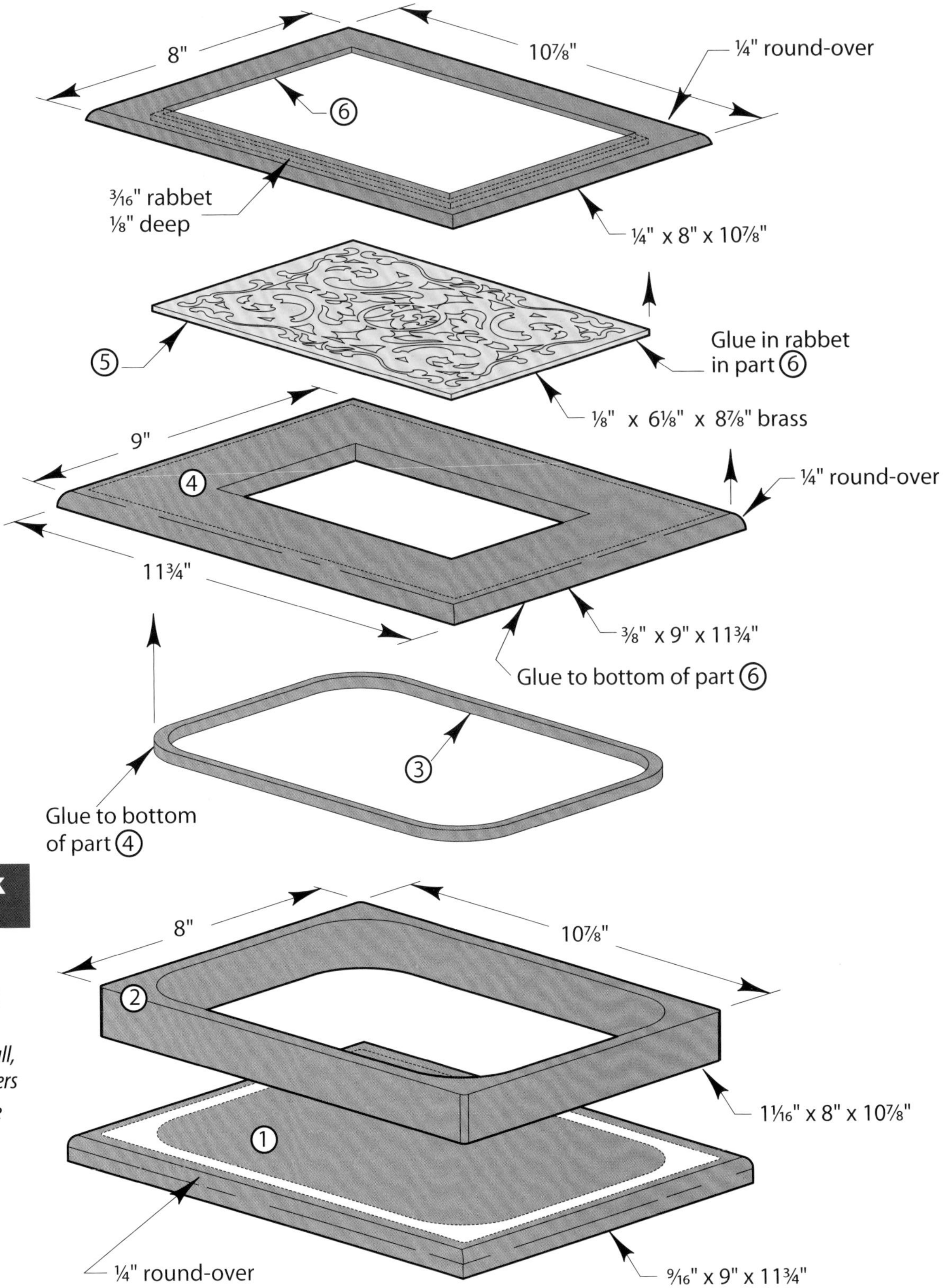
8"
10⅞"
¼" round-over
6
³⁄₁₆" rabbet
⅛" deep
¼" x 8" x 10⅞"
5
Glue in rabbet
in part 6
⅛" x 6⅛" x 8⅞" brass
9"
4
¼" round-over
11¾"
⅜" x 9" x 11¾"
Glue to bottom of part 6
3
Glue to bottom
of part 4
8"
10⅞"
2
1¹⁄₁₆" x 8" x 10⅞"
1
¼" round-over
⁹⁄₁₆" x 9" x 11¾"

Order of Work at a Glance

1. *Apply the patterns*
2. *Stack, wrap, scroll, sand, and polish the brass*
3. *Cut out the base, box wall, main lid, and top lid layers*
4. *Mark, position, and glue the lid and lid lip*
5. *Assemble and glue the main box pieces*
6. *Assemble and glue the main lid, brass pattern, and top lid*
7. *Finish the project with Danish oil*
8. *Fill the box with your favorite treasures and mementos!*

Scrolling the Brass Pattern and Monogram

Step 1: Place the brass on your piece of scrap wood. Then, wrap the stack together securely with one layer of clear packaging tape.

▲ **Step 2: Attach the pattern.** Spray the pattern with glue, or a suitable removable adhesive, and affix it to the brass plate.

Step 3: Drill the 1/16" blade entry holes.

▲ **Step 4: Cut.** Lightly spray the blade with silicon for one to two seconds. Then, cut out the pattern.

▲ **Step 5: Sand the back of the brass.** Use 600 grit and sand until all burrs are removed.

▲ **Step 6: Smooth out cutting imperfections.** Use metal files.

▲ **Step 7: Polish the brass.** If using scrap or unpolished metal, shine the piece with a rotary polishing tool with a felt or muslin rag wheel.

Making and Attaching the Lid Lip

Step 1: Cut the pieces. Apply the patterns and scroll all the walnut pieces. Sand as needed through 320 grit.

Step 2: Rout the top edges. Do layers 1, 3, and 5 with a 1/4"-radius round-over bit.

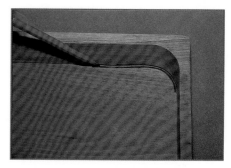

▲ **Step 3: Draw a pencil line around the top, inside edge of the box wall (layer 2).** Then, draw a 1/4" line inside this line, as shown.

Step 4: Scroll the lid lip.

Step 5: Gently round over both topside edges of the lid lip. Do this by hand to soften the edges.

Photocopy at 200% Part 5

▲ Step 6: Test fit. Turn the main lid upside down, position the box wall on the main lid, and clamp in place.

Step 7: Glue. Apply glue to the underside of lid lip and put it in place.

Step 8: Remove the wall. Without disturbing the lid lip placement, carefully remove the box wall.

Step 9: Clamp the lid lip and allow it to dry. Follow the glue manufacturer's recommendations.

Final Box Assembly and Finishing

▲ Step 1: Rout the bottom inside edge of top lid. Layer 6 should be ³⁄₁₆" wide by ³⁄₃₂" deep, or at a dimension slightly more than the thickness of your brass piece.

▲ Step 2: Square the rabbet. Use a small wood chisel or suitable equivalent to square out the corners of the rabbet cut to accommodate the brass piece.

▲ Step 3: Gently round over the top, inside edges of layers 5 and 3. Do this by hand with 220-grit sandpaper.

Step 4: Measure and mark the position of box wall (layer 2) on the base (layer 1). When measuring, use long strips of masking tape along the entire lengths of each side; pencil marks are difficult to remove.

▲ Step 5: Glue and clamp the box wall and base layers in place.

Step 6: Apply finish. Finish the main lid only on the area directly beneath the border of the brass layer. If a finish is applied to the main lid's entire surface, layer 6 will not have a good bond.

Step 7: Adhere the brass piece. Using a very thin layer of caulk, affix the brass piece to layer 5 and let it dry.

Step 8: Glue the top lid (layer 6). Glue it to layer 4 with the brass plate between them and let it dry.

Step 9: Apply the final finish. Apply six to eight coats of Danish oil to the project and allow to it dry.

Brass Scrolling Dos and Don'ts

Contrary to popular belief, brass neither is difficult to work with nor requires an expensive scroll saw to cut it as long as it is soft brass. Actual brass content of items varies significantly, so be sure the brass you are using is soft brass.

Older, single speed saws with shorter stroke lengths and pin-end-style blades may not work as smoothly with brass. The short stroke length allows the blade to overheat, and pin-end blades are too wide to turn sharp corners. However, if your saw can throttle back to about 1,000 strokes per minute and accept standard blades, then this project should be a breeze.

The following are some Dos and Don'ts I learned from my experiences during the creation of this keepsake box:

- *Always wear eye protection when drilling, cutting, or sanding brass.*
- *Clear packing tape lubricates the blade, but make sure to tape over the entire cutting surface for greater stability.*
- *Wrap all of the edges of brass in tape so you don't cut your hands.*
- *You can double the life of your blade by creating a higher working surface to take advantage of the blade's unused portion.*
- *Turn corners slowly to avoid catching the brass and lifting it off the table.*
- *Be aware that heat is generated quickly when cutting and sanding brass.*
- *Don't try to cut brass without a backer board. As you cut, the blade creates burrs on the back, which impede the movement of the piece and will scratch your table.*

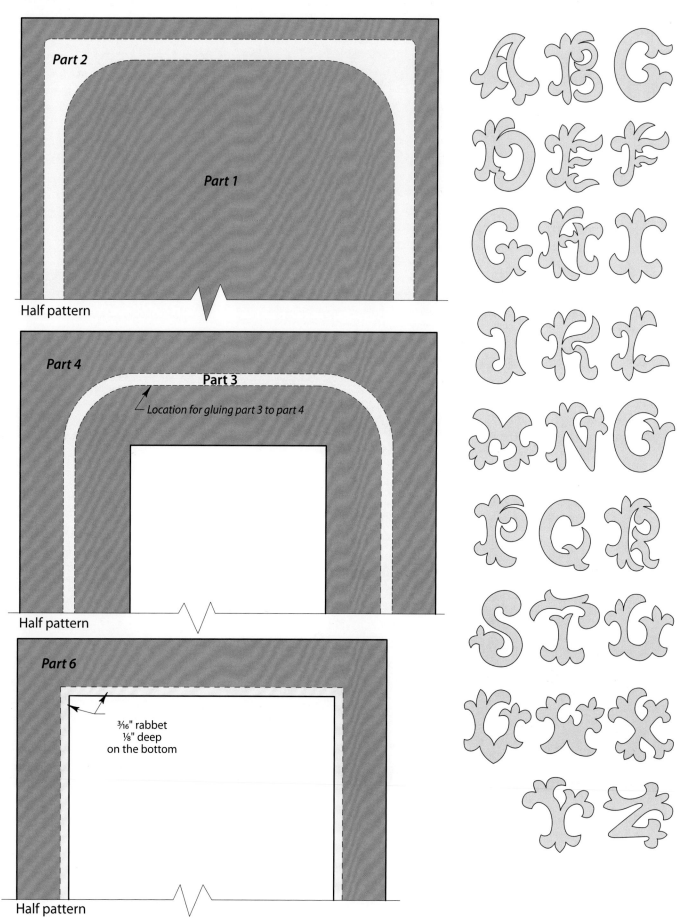

Part 2

Part 1

Half pattern

Part 4

Part 3

Location for gluing part 3 to part 4

Half pattern

Part 6

³⁄₁₆" rabbet
⅛" deep
on the bottom

Half pattern

Photocopy at 200%

Holiday Card Holder

Fretwork tote organizes cards and mail in style

By John A. Nelson
Cut by Ben Fink

This Victorian-inspired basket is perfect for displaying Christmas cards. When the season is over, use the tote to collect mail, sewing supplies, remote controls, or a variety of other items.

You can adjust the design to suit your needs. It makes a beautiful decorative caddy for antique bottles or perfumes and lotions. Enlarge the pattern 130% to hold magazines. If you alter the dimensions of the pattern, you will need to manually adjust the tab slots. Be sure to account for variations in the thickness of your material.

Cut the pieces from your wood of choice. You can stack cut the end and side panels. Leave the slots slightly undersized. Sand or file the slots to accommodate the tabs for a perfect fit. The tabs and slots are coded by letter for easy assembly.

Apply your finish of choice. I use Danish oil. You can glue the tabs into the slots or create a tight joint with the sanding technique mentioned above. If the tabs are not glued in place, the basket can be disassembled for storage.

Materials & Tools

Materials:
- 2 pieces ¼" x 5½" x 9½" mimosa or wood of choice (end panels)
- 2 pieces ¼" x 3¾" x 10⅛" mimosa or wood of choice (side panels)
- ¼" x 1¾" x 10⅛" mimosa or wood of choice (bottom panel)
- ¼" x 4" x 10⅛" mimosa or wood of choice (handle)
- Wood glue (optional)
- Assorted grits of sandpaper up to 220 grit
- Danish oil or finish of choice

Tools:
- #3 reverse-tooth blades or blades of choice
- Drill with ⅟₁₆"-diameter drill bit
- Sander (optional)
- File
- Rags or brushes to apply finish (optional)

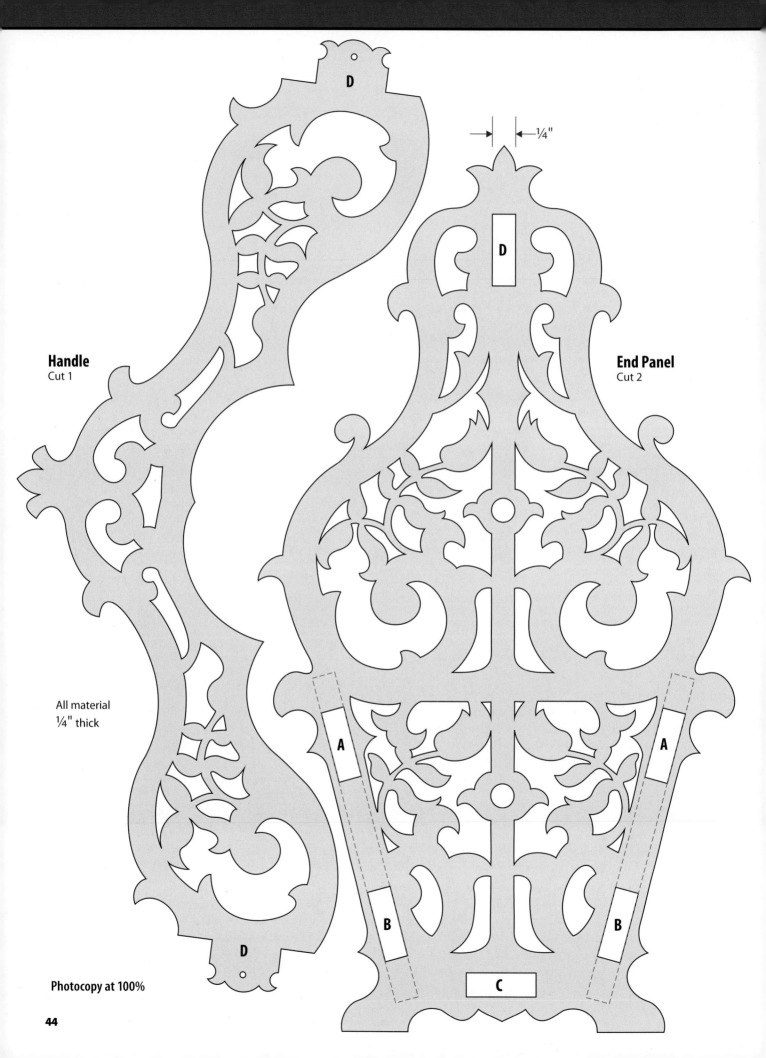

Handle
Cut 1

All material
¼" thick

Photocopy at 100%

44

¼"

End Panel
Cut 2

All holes 1/16" dia.

A   B   C   1/4"

Side Panel
Cut 2

A   B   C   1/4"

Photocopy at 100%

Bottom
Cut 1

Segmentation and Intarsia Boxes

Intarsia is popular for creating hanging art, but it also makes a great embellishment in box making. Because segmentation is similar to intarsia, it too can be a great addition to any box project. Try the boxes featured in this section or you can even modify your favorite intarsia or segmentation pattern into a box using the tips and techniques included here.

Petal-Perfect Rose Box,
by Robert Ardizzoni, page 48.

Petal-Perfect Rose Box

Basic technique turns any design into a custom keepsake box

By Robert Ardizzoni

The rose is a classic symbol of love and the flagship of the flower garden. I'm always a little saddened when the first cool days of autumn are on the horizon. I was looking for a way to bring summer inside all year long. This perennial blossom doesn't have the delightful scent of a real rose, but it does function as a keepsake box and makes a beautiful gift.

I first crafted the rose intarsia as a wall hanging, mounted on 1/8"-thick birch plywood with a handmade frame, but my wife said it was too nice to hang on the wall. She asked me to make one to put on the coffee table and later suggested I make it into a box.

Preserve the romance of summer with this timeless rose intarsia.

1

Transfer the center pattern to the wood. Make a photocopy of the pattern and shade the back with a soft lead pencil. Position the pattern over the blank, and trace along the lines of petals 1 to 9 with a red ballpoint pen, so you can see where you have already traced.

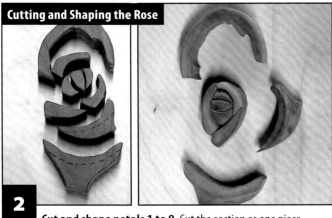

Cutting and Shaping the Rose

2 **Cut and shape petals 1 to 9.** Cut the section as one piece with a #12 blade. Then, separate the petals with a #2 blade. Shape the petals with a sander, using the arrows on the pattern as a guide. Work toward the center. Use 350-grit sandpaper to remove any scratches.

3 **Glue the center section together.** Apply masking tape to the edges. Then, spray the face of the petals with a coat of lacquer. The lacquer prevents glue from adhering to the face of the intarsia. Remove the masking tape, apply glue to the edges, and glue the petals together.

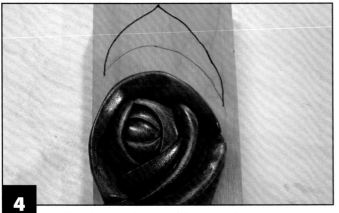

4 **Cut the other petals.** Start with petal 10. Trace the pattern onto your stock. Then, align the center section and trace the adjoining line with a red pen. Cut the piece with a #12 blade; cut outside the red line and sand up to it for a perfect fit. Use the same process to cut the other pieces.

5 **Shape the remaining petals and leaves.** Reduce the thickness using the chart as a guide (see page 51). Shape the pieces, using the arrows as a guide. Tape and lacquer the pieces. When dry, remove the tape and glue petals 10 to 14 to the center section. Set the other pieces aside.

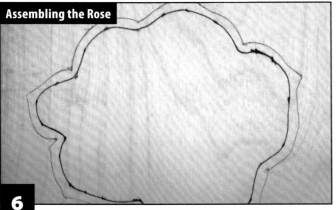

Assembling the Rose

6 **Create the lid backing board.** Place the center assembly on ⅛"-thick Baltic birch plywood and position the remaining petals around it. Trace the rose with a red pen. Make a black line ³⁄₁₆" in from the red line. Drill a blade entry hole between the lines and cut along the black line.

7 **Glue the petals to the backing board.** Align all of the pieces on the backing board, and then remove the loose petals. Trace the position of the center assembly, and then glue it in place. Allow the glue to set. Then, glue petals 15 through 18 in place. Allow the glue to dry overnight.

Creating the Box

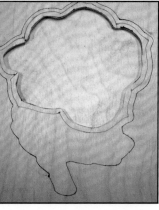

8 **Create the box template.** Position the lid assembly back in the hole in the plywood. Place the stem and leaves in position. Trace around the entire piece. I place a pen inside a ¼"-diameter washer for consistent spacing. Cut the box template and smooth the outside perimeter only.

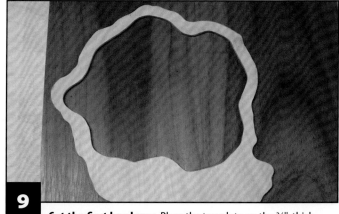

9 **Cut the first box layer.** Place the template on the ¾"-thick walnut and trace the inside and outside. Cut ¹⁄₆₄" outside the perimeter and ¹⁄₆₄" inside the lid area. Sand to the lines. I use a spindle sander. Check the fit of the lid assembly and sand the box to fit. Allow extra space for the flocking paint.

10 **Cut the second box layer.** Remove any burrs from the first layer with 220-grit sandpaper. Do not round over the edge. Trace around the top layer for the second layer. Use the same techniques from Step 9 to cut and shape the second layer. Then, glue and clamp the two layers together.

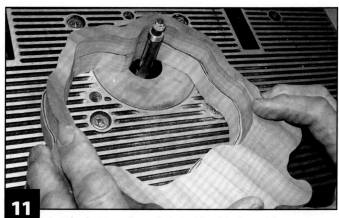

11 **Cut the bottom.** Smooth the inside of the box with a router and a flush-trim bit. Then, sand the inside with a spindle sander. Trace the perimeter of the sides onto ¼"-thick walnut. Cut along the line; then, glue and clamp the bottom to the sides. Smooth and sand the perimeter.

Finishing the Box

12 **Apply the finish.** Place the stem and leaves on the box sides, but do not glue them down. Spray several coats of lacquer over the entire piece. When the lacquer is dry, glue the stem and leaves in place where there is no obvious lacquer. Replace the lid and apply another coat of lacquer.

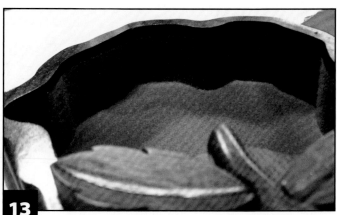

13 **Flock the inside of the box.** Paint the edge of the lid bottom and ⅛" down the insides of the box with flocking paint and dry overnight. Mask off the top ⅛" of the box. Follow the manufacturer's instructions to flock the inside of the box and the lid backing. Attach felt feet to the bottom of the box.

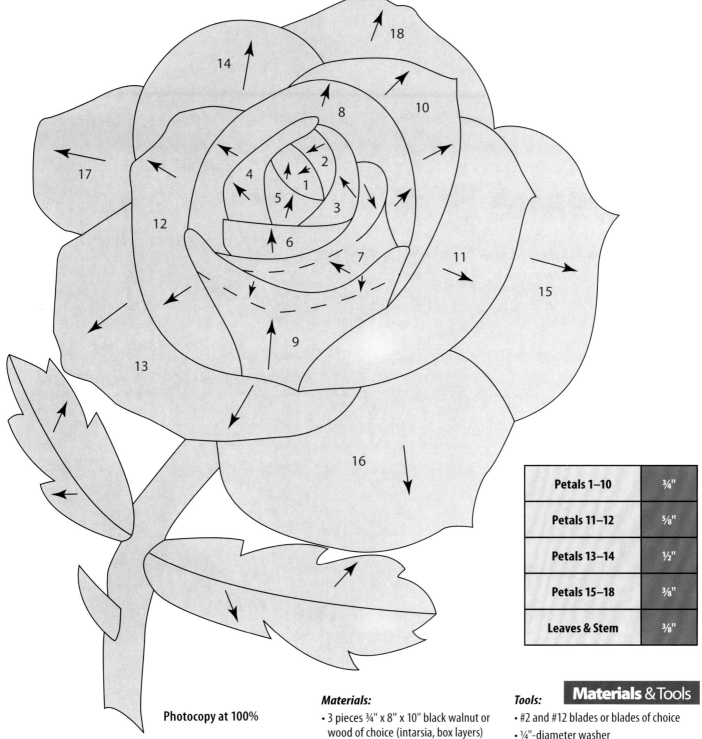

Petals 1–10	¾"
Petals 11–12	⅝"
Petals 13–14	½"
Petals 15–18	⅜"
Leaves & Stem	⅜"

Photocopy at 100%

Materials & Tools

Materials:
- 3 pieces ¾" x 8" x 10" black walnut or wood of choice (intarsia, box layers)
- ¼" x 8" x 10" black walnut or matching wood of choice (box bottom)
- ⅛" x 8" x 10" Baltic birch plywood (box lid backing, box layer template)
- Wood glue or glue of choice
- Sandpaper, 220 and 350 grits
- Spray lacquer
- Flocking kit (available from most woodworking suppliers)
- Masking tape
- Felt pads

Tools:
- #2 and #12 blades or blades of choice
- ¼"-diameter washer
- Router with flush-trim bit
- Sander of choice (I use a spindle sander, a belt sander, and a rotary power carver)
- Drill with 1/16"- and 3/16"-diameter bits
- Assorted clamps
- #2 pencil
- Red and black ballpoint pens

Eagle Keepsake Box

Straightforward project is ideal for beginners

By Paul Meisel

This box makes an attractive place for valuable keepsakes. The eagle decorating the top can be made as segmentation or intarsia. Both the box and eagle are easy to cut and assemble, so even beginners can successfully complete the project. Select a combination of light and dark wood for the eagle appliqué, or simplify the design by cutting all of the parts from ¼"-thick cherry and staining the dark segments.

Building the Box
Step 1: Cut the box sides. Use a table saw to rip the ½"-thick stock to 3¾"-wide. This will be used for the box front, back, and sides.

Step 2: Cut the mitered corners. Set the miter saw to cut at a 45° angle and cut the front and back to 10¾" long. Cut the sides to 5" long. Dry fit the four pieces together and check the fit.

Step 3: Assemble the box sides. Glue and clamp the front, back, and side pieces together. I use a strap clamp. Use a square to check that the assembly is square and allow the glue to dry.

Step 4: Separate the lid from the sides. Set the blade height on your table saw to ⅝". Set the rip fence ¾" from the blade and cut all around

the glue-up to separate the lid frame from the box frame.

Step 5: Drill pilot holes for the hinges and lid support screws. Drill the ¹⁄₁₆"-diameter holes now because they will be difficult to drill after the top and bottom are attached.

Step 6: Cut the top and bottom. You may need to edge glue two ¼" x 3" x 24" boards together to get the required width. Cut the pieces to 5¼" x 11". Sand the edges until smooth and slightly rounded.

Step 7: Assemble the box. Center the box frame on the bottom stock and center the lid frame on the top stock. Attach the top and bottom with wood glue. Make sure the lid and sides are both centered correctly and line up with each other. Allow the glue to dry. Then, install the hinges and lid support.

The Eagle Embellishment
Step 8: Transfer the pattern to your stock. For the intarsia version, select the direction of grain you prefer for each piece. I arrange the grain of the walnut parts to follow the spread of the wings, simulating feathers. The grain on the remaining parts was left in a vertical direction.

Step 9: Cut the parts. Use a #2 reverse-skip-tooth blade. Round over the edges as desired. Arrange the pieces of the eagle so they are centered on the top of the box, and glue them in place.

Finish the Box
▲ **Step 10: Apply the finish.** Remove the hinges and lid support and brush on a coat of sanding sealer. When the sealer is dry, sand lightly with 220-grit sandpaper. Remove any dust, and then apply a coat of polyurethane varnish.

Step 11: Line the box. Use scissors to cut the pressure-sensitive felt to size. Remove the backing paper and press the felt into place. Replace the hinges and lid support.

Materials & Tools

Materials:

- ½" x 3¾" x 36" oak (sides)
- 2 pieces ¼" x 3" x 24" oak or 1 piece ¼" x 6" x 24" oak (lid and bottom)
- ¼" x 3½" x 9⅝" wood of choice (eagle)
- Brass hinges & lid support kit with screws
- 2 each 9" x 12" pressure-sensitive green felt
- Sanding sealer
- Assorted stains of choice (optional)
- Polyurethane varnish
- Sandpaper, 220 grit
- Wood glue

Tools:

- Table saw
- Miter saw
- #2 reverse-skip-tooth blades or blades of choice
- #0 Phillips screwdriver (to install hinges and lid support)
- Drill with ⅟₁₆"-diameter drill bit
- Scissors
- Strap clamp or clamps of choice
- Drum sander with 80- and 120-grit sleeves (to shape intarsia and segmentation)
- Paintbrushes

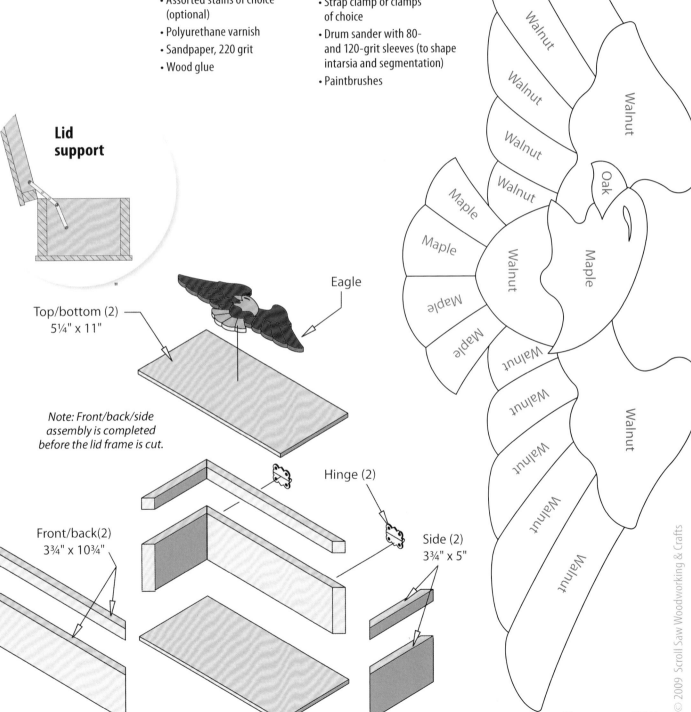

Lid support

Top/bottom (2)
5¼" x 11"

Eagle

Note: Front/back/side assembly is completed before the lid frame is cut.

Front/back(2)
3¾" x 10¾"

Hinge (2)

Side (2)
3¾" x 5"

Walnut · Walnut · Walnut · Walnut · Walnut · Oak · Maple · Maple · Walnut · Maple · Maple · Maple · Maple · Walnut · Walnut · Walnut · Walnut · Walnut · Walnut

Photocopy at 100%

Fantasy Keepsake Boxes

Segmentation techniques and brilliant colors breathe life into these boxes

*By Sue Chrestensen
Based on designs
by Lora S. Irish*

Popular gift and sale items, these embellished boxes look great whether you choose to highlight the natural wood or personalize them with color.

A Note on Designs

I have had the pleasure of making these two projects from Lora S. Irish's magnificent art. The dragon box is from the Great Book of Dragon Patterns; *the fairy is a compilation of two patterns from the* Great Book of Fairy Patterns. *The manner in which the boxes were made is the result of standard segmentation techniques and my imagination.*

The work would be considered a derivative of Lora's copyrighted art. She maintains that copyright and these patterns are presented with her consent.

Segmentation and stack cutting techniques make these boxes much easier to create than they look. They are a great way to keep small items organized and make a perfect gift for teens. They are also easy to customize by changing the colors, raising and lowering different pieces, or by using traditional intarsia techniques to take advantage of interesting grains or wood colors.

Having never met one, I imagine dragons to be colorful creatures. It was helpful in doing this project to color some extra copies of the pattern before beginning to stain this project—I looked at various options and color combinations, and then made my choice. Your dragon might be a totally different color. Just have fun with whatever decision you make—it's your imagination and vision.

I've also included a pattern for a fairy box. It uses almost the same techniques.

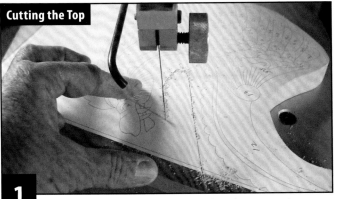

Cutting the Top

1 **Prepare your blanks.** Make sure the boards are smooth and flat. Attach the pattern using your method of choice. I put blue painter's tape on the wood and apply temporary bond spray adhesive to the pattern. Then, I press the pattern firmly onto the wood. Remove the extra wood from around the pattern.

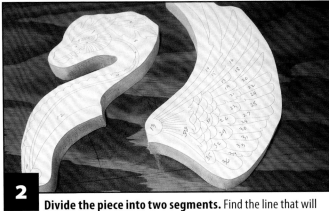

2 **Divide the piece into two segments.** Find the line that will allow you to cut the project into manageable sections. Keep a small piece of fine sandpaper handy to remove any burrs or jagged edges left by the blade.

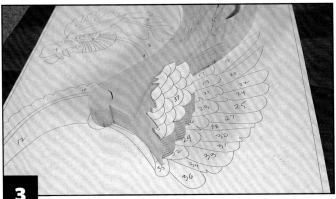

3 **Cut out the pieces.** Write the number of each piece on the bottom as you cut it. Then, place it in the corresponding location on the master pattern. Transfer the lines onto the flowery part under the dragon's wings by pressing hard with a pen to leave an indentation behind. I made more indentations into the wood, using Lora's pattern as a guide. Remove the tape and patterns on all the pieces except the wings, head, and the feathers. The longer the tape remains on the wood, the more difficult it is to remove.

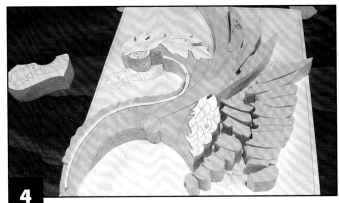

4 **Create a pattern for the remaining pieces.** Place the pieces tightly together on the master pattern—you will notice that the cut dragon is slightly smaller than the original pattern. This is because of the saw kerf. Secure all of the pieces together with masking tape, move them to the pine box sides piece, and trace around the piece. Alternatively, you can trace the pieces onto a piece of paper and attach that paper to the box sides piece using spray adhesive, or even use a copy of the original pattern and cut inside the lines.

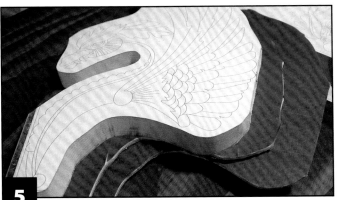

5 **Prepare the backer board, box sides, and the box bottom for stack cutting.** Cover both sides of one of the 1/8"-thick pieces of Baltic birch plywood with blue painter's tape. Cover one side of the pine board and the other 1/8"-thick piece of plywood. Apply spray adhesive to the tape, and press the pieces together, making sure the pine is on top and the plywood with tape on both sides is in the middle. If you did not trace your pattern on the pine, tape the other side and apply the pattern, using spray adhesive.

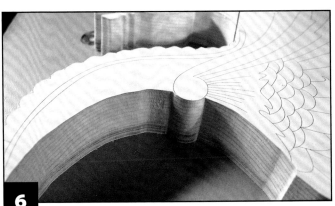

6 **Cut out the backer board, box bottom, and the box sides.** Use the same techniques explained above to cut out ONLY the outline of the dragon on all three pieces at the same time. As soon as you finish cutting these pieces, separate them. I have found it gets more difficult to separate pieces when they are left attached.

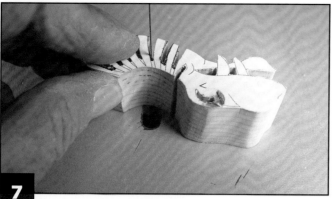

7 **Cut the details in the face.** Set the backer board and the box sides aside and go back to the segments cut in Step 3. Drill blade entry holes between the dragon's teeth and at the back of its mouth. Cut out and remove the wood from the area under the dragon's eye. This fret-style removal of wood in combination with a segmented piece adds to the overall look of this project. The eye is composed of three very small pieces—cut it out carefully.

8 **Add details to the leaves over the dragon's head.** Details can be added to the project in a variety of ways. A hand-held rotary tool has many possibilities and accessories that can be used to detail a project—from the details in a feather to the lines on a leaf. Again, it is in the eye of the person making the project. Creativity and giving yourself permission to experiment is key.

Cutting the Sides

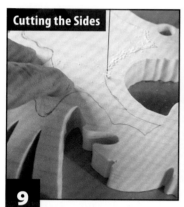

9 **Prepare the box sides.** Drill a ³⁄₈" hole for the dowel as shown on the pattern. Draw a line approximately ½" in from the outside of the dragon following its contours in the ¾"-thick pine for the box sides. Keep in mind that really narrow areas aren't usable. This is the area to be cut out and removed forming the "box" area. Drill a blade entry hole wherever it is convenient. Cut out the inside of the box.

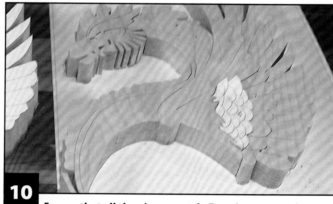

10 **Ensure that all the pieces match.** Tape the segmented pieces together and place them on the cut backer board. Center the pieces and match them up to the edges. Compare this to the box side and box bottom. Sand any areas that don't match up smoothly.

Sanding the Dragon

11 **Sand, shim, and shape the pieces.** Start by sanding the edges of all the pieces to give the project a finished look. You can also use a belt sander to reduce the thicknesses of pieces to add depth and dimension. You want the pieces to flow together but still be distinct. If you want some pieces to be higher than others, add a small shim below them. You can also use a rotary carving tool to add texture, (such as adding folds to the fairy's dress in the alternate pattern).

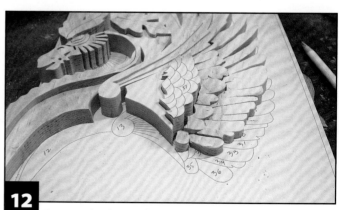

12 **Prepare the dragon for staining.** Sand all the pieces with progressively finer sandpaper up to 220 grit. The end grain often comes out darker when stained the same color. One way to help even the color out is to sand the end grain to a higher grit—sand the end grain to 400 or 600 grit.

Assembling and finishing

13 **Glue the box bottom to the box sides.** Apply a thin coat of wood glue to the bottom of the box sides, place the box bottom in place, and clamp overnight.

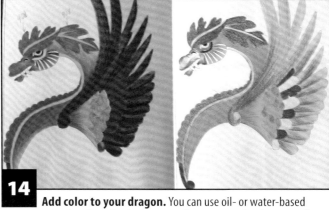

14 **Add color to your dragon.** You can use oil- or water-based stains, leather dyes, food coloring, and even paint. Combining and experimenting with color is half the fun. It is also important to know that sanding away color, leaving just a hint that it had been there, can add a great highlight to an area. Just be sure to let the stain dry, and lightly sand between coats of varnish. Also, stain both of the backer boards and the box sides. A piece of brown paper bag can be used as a sandpaper alternative and is the equivalent of 1600-grit sandpaper. It works wonderfully on acrylic paint. Use your finish of choice on the box.

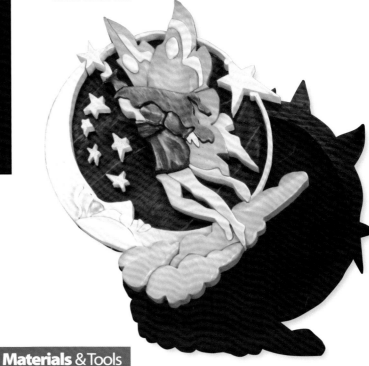

15 **Glue the segmentation pieces down onto the backer board.** Start by applying a light coat of glue to one piece. Clamp this piece in place until it is dry. Then, work your way out from there. As you glue more pieces around the first piece, add weights or clamp them in place to prevent them from moving. Drill a hole halfway through the segmented lid and its backer board the same size as your dowel. Cut the dowel to fit, letting the top of the box lie flat. Glue the dowel into the bottom box. When finished, sign and date your work.

Materials:
- 2 pieces 1" x 10" x 12" pine (segmentation and box sides)
- 2 pieces ⅛" x 10" x 12" Baltic birch plywood (backer board and box bottom)
- Temporary bond spray adhesive
- Blue painter's tape
- Fine-point marker
- Wood glue of choice (I useTitebond III)
- Sandpaper, 120, 150, 220, and 400 to 600 grits
- Brown paper bag (to sand down some finishes)
- Varnish

- ⅜"-diameter x 2" section of dowel
- Stains or paints of choice

Materials & Tools

Tools:
- # 2, #5, and #7 reverse-tooth blades or blades of choice
- Belt sander (optional for sanding down segmentation pieces)
- Rotary tool (optional for sanding or shaping segmentation pieces)
- Drill or drill press
- ¹⁄₃₂"-diameter drill bit
- ⅜"-diameter drill bit

TIP **USING A THIN COAT OF GLUE**

Because the segmentation pieces are not really structural, a very light, thin coat of glue will hold the piece firmly. Using a light coat of glue also means that the piece will be less likely to move.

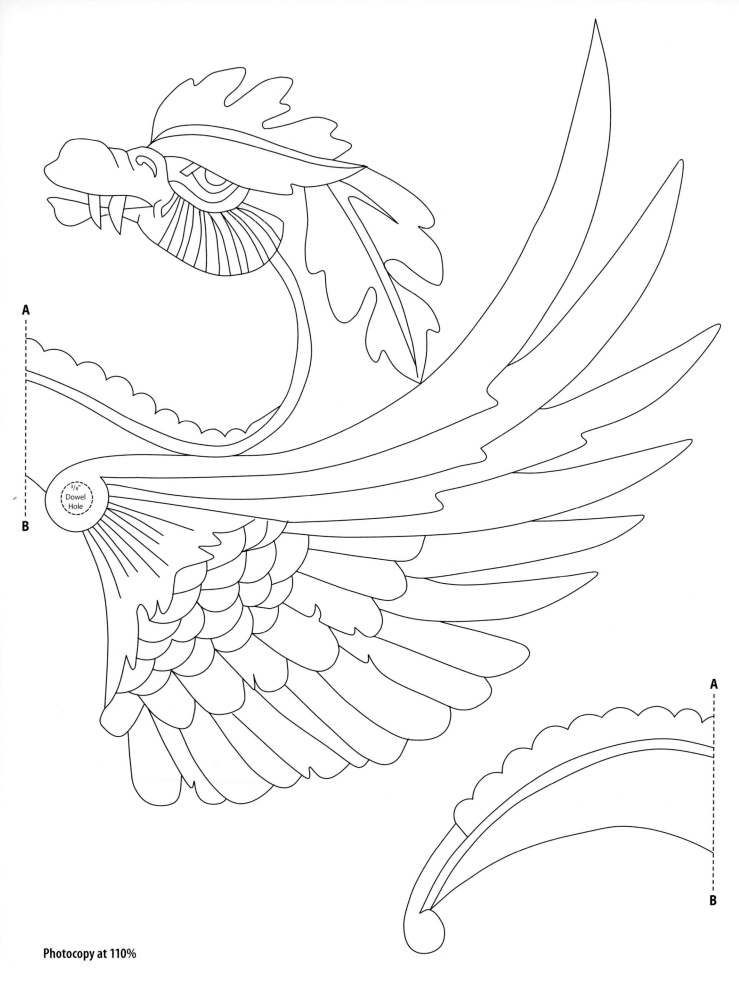

Photocopy at 110%

³/₈"
Dowel
Hole

Photocopy at 110%

Hanging Backpack Box

Segmented sections and rich colors create a realistic look

By Sue Chrestensen

Materials & Tools

Materials:
- 1" x 12" x 36" pine (segmented lid and box sides)
- ⅛" x 12" x 24" Baltic birch plywood (backer board and box bottom)
- ½" x 2" x 24" wood of choice (hanging board for pegs)
- 3 wooden shaker pegs, ½"-diameter x 2"
- ¼"-diameter dowel
- Latch hook
- Temporary bond spray adhesive
- Blue painter's tape
- Marker (to number the pieces)
- Wood glue
- Sandpaper, 120, 150, & 220 grits
- Stain or dye to color the wood (optional)
- Assorted paints
- Varnish (optional)

Tools:
- #5 reverse-tooth blades or blades of choice
- ½"- and ¹⁄₃₂"-diameter drill bit
- Belt sander (optional to thin down stock)
- Rotary tool and assorted carving burrs (optional to texture the segmentation)
- Drill or drill press

This coat rack is a fun and functional project that looks great in a hallway or kid's bedroom. The inside of the backpack can have a mirror, shelves, or hooks to hang jewelry.

The outside of the backpack can be any color, and any flaws in the wood will just give it a used look. Imagine a well-worn, often-used backpack—add some dents and curves where you think they belong and give this project character and unique qualities based on your imagination.

Step 1: Cut around the perimeter of the pattern. Then, find the interior lines that will let you divide the piece into manageable sections. I cut along the flap line. Keep a small piece of sandpaper handy to remove any burrs generated by the cutting.

Step 2: Cut out the segmentation pieces. Label a master copy of the pattern and the bottom of each piece with a number for easy assembly. Remove the pattern—the longer the pattern remains on the wood, the more difficult it is to remove. Place each piece in the corresponding location on the master pattern.

Step 3: Make a template and cut out the backer board. Use the segmentation pieces to draw the template for the backer board. The hanging strap portion of the segmentation is not attached to the top backer board but is glued directly to the box sides. Do not include this section in your pattern for the backer board.

Step 4: Glue and clamp two pieces of pine together for the box sides. Temporarily stack a piece of plywood to the bottom of this section for the box bottom. Transfer a complete pattern to this blank. Cut around the outside of the pattern and the inside of the hanging strap.

Step 5: Cut the inside of the box. Remove the plywood layer and the pattern from the pine box sides. Draw a line approximately ½" inside the perimeter of the pine box sides blank. Drill a blade entry hole, insert your blade of choice, and cut out the inside of the box. Glue and clamp the plywood box bottom onto the back of the sides, let it dry, and sand the assembly for a good fit.

Step 6: Shape the segmentation pieces. Use a hand-held rotary tool or a power sander, or shape the sections by hand sanding. Remove a fair amount of wood from the pockets and flap on the backpack. Sand these areas smooth. This gives the appearance of a fold and implies that the leather is soft. Sanding the edges of all of the pieces gives the project a finished and coordinated look; the pieces flow together, yet are very distinct. Shape the hanging strap segmentation pieces at this time as well.

Step 7: Position the segmentation pieces on the backer board. Arrange the pieces on the backer board and cut shims for any sections you would like to raise. Shims should only be used on inside pieces. You do not want them to show and detract from the project. Complete any final shaping of the segmentation pieces to achieve a natural flow.

Step 8: Color and finish the project. Finishes on any project are a matter of personal choice. The key is to put as much energy and effort into the finishing as you did the rest of the project. I use leather dyes to color my backpack. To distress the finish, sand different spots with 220-grit sandpaper to make some lighter areas. Use metallic paint for the buckles and acrylic washes for the pencils. Finish the base of the box as well.

Step 9: Glue the segmentation pieces to the backer board. Arrange all the pieces on the plywood backer. Remove one inside piece, apply a small amount of wood glue, and return it to the original position. Clamp the piece in place, and allow it to dry overnight. Continue outward from the center piece, removing, gluing, and clamping pieces from the inside toward the perimeter. Glue the segmented pieces for the hanging strap directly on the box sides.

Step 10: Assemble the box. Drill the hole for the dowel that will hold the top to the box. Drill a hole the same diameter as your dowel halfway through the pine box and halfway through the segmented portion and backer board of the lid. Cut the dowel to fit, letting the top of the box lie flat. Glue the dowel into the bottom box. Attach the latch hook onto the left side of the box with small screws. Sign the back of your project.

Step 11: Create the peg rack. You can use a commercial peg rack or create your own. Drill holes the same diameter as your pegs into a length of wood and glue the pegs into the holes. Attach a hanger to the back of the coat rack board. Hang the backpack on the coat rack board with the peg going through the strap opening on the upper left-hand corner.

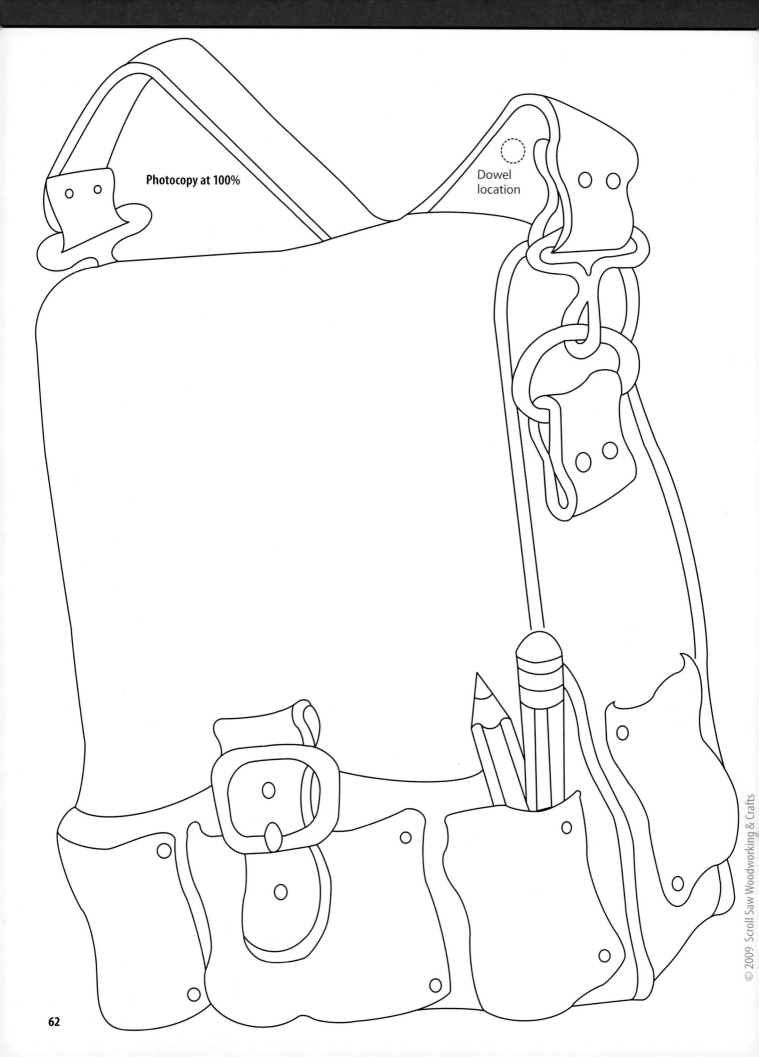

Photocopy at 100%

Dowel location

Dragon Chest

Original designs and vivid colors are highlights of this distinct box

By Kenneth Campbell

I crafted this project to meet my personal preferences and never imagined it would be awarded the grand prize in *SSW&C*'s Best Project Design Contest. When I read about the contest, I decided to enter the chest just for fun. The dragon design started out as a drawing that had nothing to do with woodworking. I thought it would be fun to design a dragon tattoo. So I started doodling and ended up with a sketch of the main dragon that adorns the lid.

Once the dragon design was on paper, it just seemed natural to cut the design out of wood. I transferred the image to ¼"-thick poplar and cut it out. I had no idea what I would do with the cutout at that point, but I decided to add some texture. As I worked on the dragon, the idea of a minichest slowly took shape, and I incorporated elements of the main design in the trim work and box sides. I wanted to showcase the dragon design and decided to stain it black and add a bright backing board for contrast. I'm very pleased with the end result and am thrilled that my project was chosen as the contest winner.

Step 1: Transfer the patterns to the blanks. Apply spray adhesive to the backs of the patterns, and position them on the blanks.

Step 2: Prepare the frame overlay pieces for stack cutting. The long sides and short sides are mirror images of each other, so when you stack them together, be sure the sides of the wood you want to be the bottoms are facing each other. Wrap blue painter's tape around the edges to hold the stack together. I cut the pieces to size and cut the miters with a miter saw. Note that not all of the patterns are an equal width.

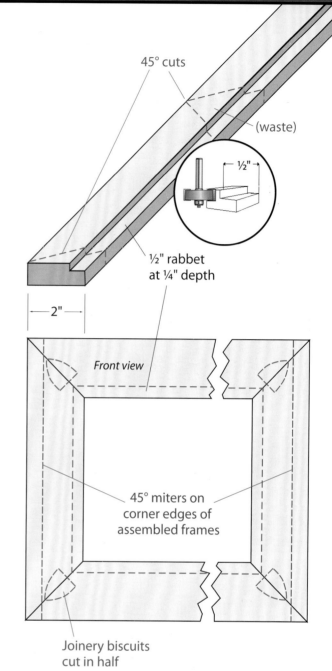

45° cuts

(waste)

½"

½" rabbet at ¼" depth

2"

Front view

45° miters on corner edges of assembled frames

Joinery biscuits cut in half

▲ **Step 3: Cut out the patterns.** Drill blade entry holes where needed with a ⅛"-diameter drill bit. Then, cut out the pieces using your blade of choice.

Step 4: Cut the main dragon designs. I use a flexible shaft tool with 120-grit sanding drums to add texture. These will be affixed to the padauk after the box is assembled.

Step 5: Finish the dragon designs. Hand sand the pieces with 100-, 150-, and 220-grit sandpaper. Stain them with black India ink.

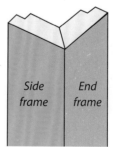

Side frame

End frame

Section view

Miters on the assembled end and side frames will join at the corners. The addition of the bottom panel forms the structure of the box.

Step 6: Cut the box frame parts. Cut three pieces of poplar to ¾" x 2" x 8'. Then, cut a ½"-wide x ¼"-deep rabbet on one side of each piece, (see Box Frame Construction). I use a router and rabbet bit. Cut the sections to length at a 45° angle.

Step 7: Cut the panels from ¼"-thick poplar. Use the materials list as a guide.

Step 8: Assemble the frames. Cut biscuit slots on the mitered ends of all of the frame pieces. Since the wood is only 2" or 2¼" wide, cut the biscuits in half. You can also use dowels or splines. Apply glue to the biscuits and miters and clamp them together until dry. When complete, you will have four box side frames.

Step 9: Cut the miters on the frame parts. Use a miter saw to cut a 45° miter on the sides. The top and bottom of the frame will remain square.

Step 10: Add the panels. Glue the poplar panels into the frames.

Step 11: Assemble the box. Cut the box bottom to size noted in the materials list. Assemble the box, using biscuits to strengthen the miter joints where the sides come together and where the sides meet the bottom.

▲ **Step 12: Glue the fretwork designs over the poplar frame pieces.** Be sure to position the wider side panel border side pieces so they overhang the short sides by ¼". This keeps the box corners in proportion.

Step 13: Cut the lid frame. The upper framework of the lid is cut from commercial molding. For the lower framework, rip a piece of ¾" x 2" x 8' poplar to a width

of 1¾" so the upper framework overhangs the lower portion (see Box Lid Construction). Use an ogee bit to rout a decorative edge along the length of the poplar. Apply wood glue to the top of the poplar and align the back edge of the molding and poplar. Clamp them together until dry. Cut the pieces to length using 45° miters on both ends. Cut the lid guide to size.

Step 14: Assemble the lid. Cut the lid panel to size, and glue the frame pieces to it using biscuit joints to add strength where the panel meets the frame and where the frame pieces join. The bottom of the panel should be approximately ¼" up from the bottom edge of the frame. Glue the bottom lid guide to the underside of the panel.

▲ **Step 15: Sand the poplar frames and fretwork overlays.** Start with 120 grit, and move on to 220 grit.

▲ **Step 16: Stain the poplar frames and fretwork with black India ink.** Tape off the inner panels and apply a clear, satin wood finish to the stained areas. Cut the feet, stain them, and glue them to the bottom.

Step 17: Cut the padauk panels. You may need to edge-glue the padauk to make the larger panels. Sand them with 220-grit sandpaper. Apply a high-gloss, clear lacquer.

Step 18: Glue the panels in place. After the padauk is in place, cut and stain 1"-wide strips of poplar to hide the layers of wood on the inner edges of the frame pieces.

▲ Step 19: Glue the dragon designs to the box. Use two-part epoxy since both the padauk and poplar have already been finished.

Box Lid Construction

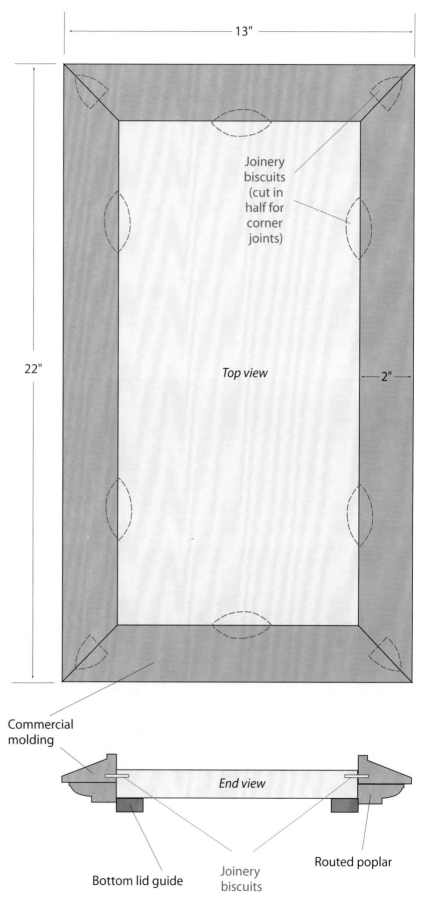

13"

22"

Joinery biscuits (cut in half for corner joints)

Top view

2"

Commercial molding

End view

Bottom lid guide

Joinery biscuits

Routed poplar

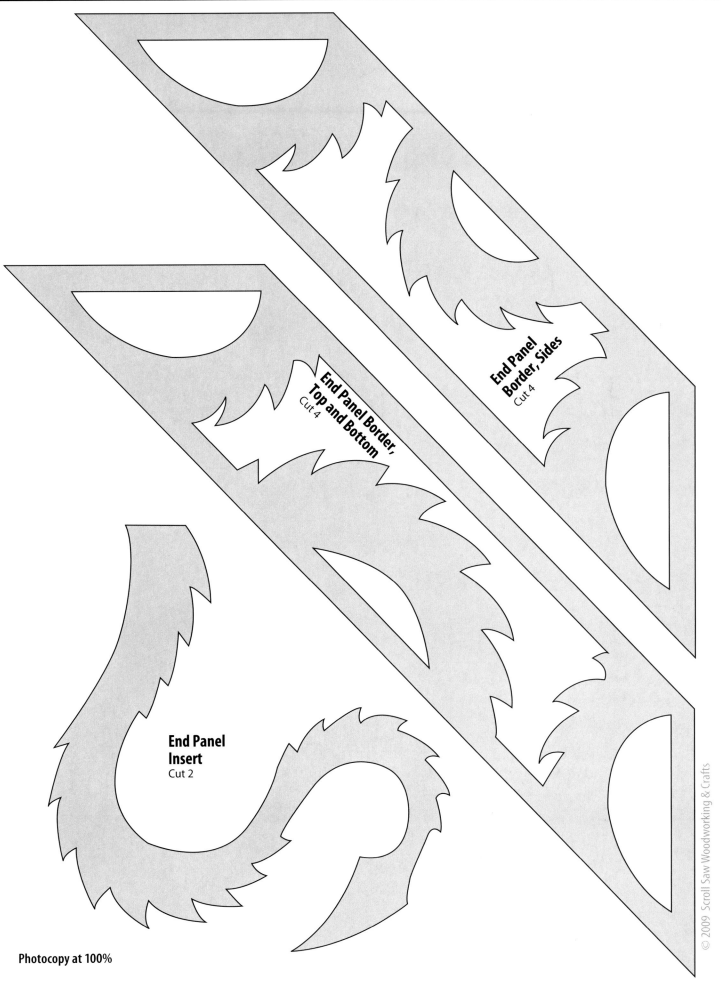

End Panel
Border, Sides
Cut 4

End Panel Border,
Top and Bottom
Cut 4

**End Panel
Insert**
Cut 2

Photocopy at 100%

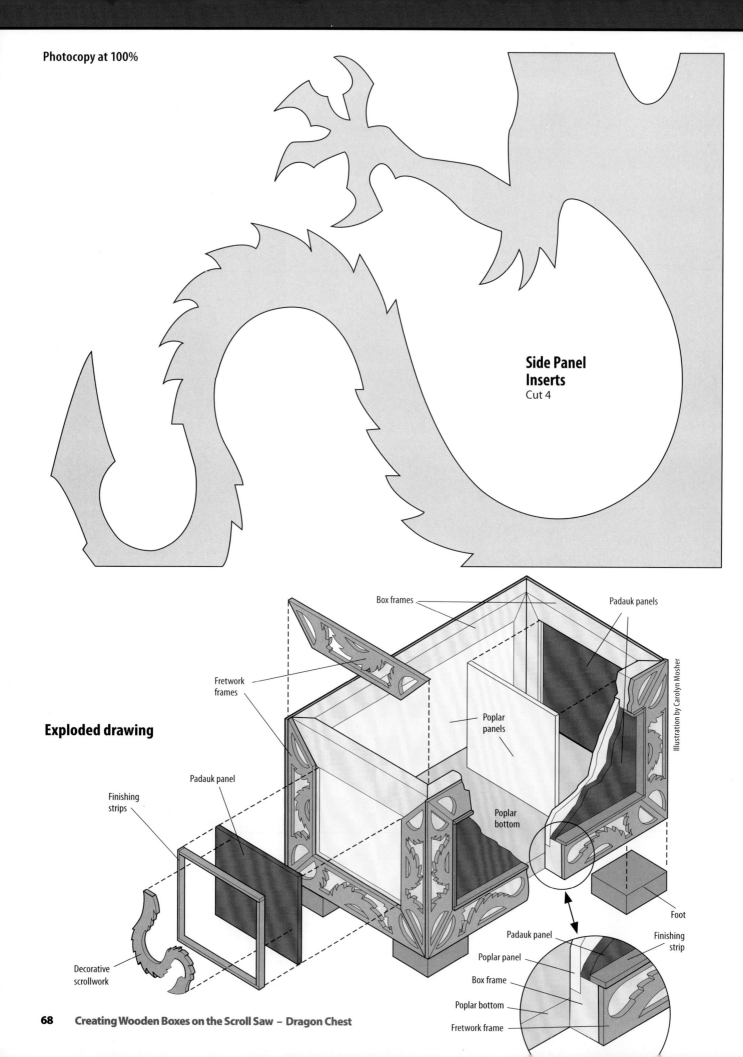

Side Panel Inserts
Cut 4

Exploded drawing

Box frames

Padauk panels

Fretwork frames

Poplar panels

Padauk panel

Poplar bottom

Finishing strips

Padauk panel

Decorative scrollwork

Foot

Illustration by Carolyn Mosher

Padauk panel

Finishing strip

Poplar panel

Box frame

Poplar bottom

Fretwork frame

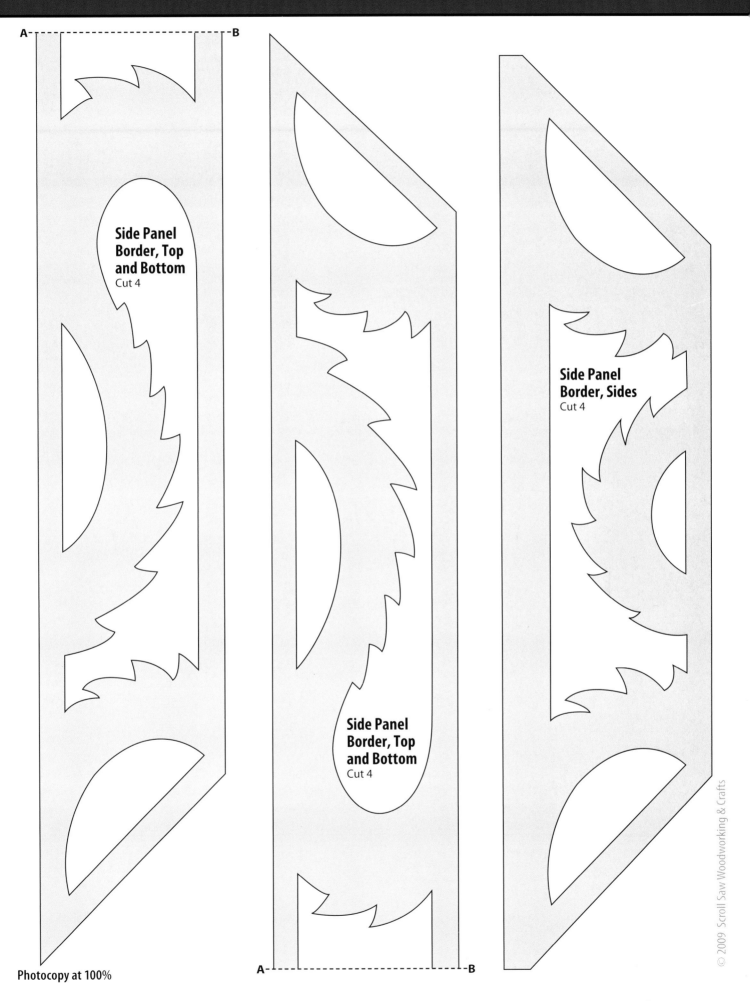

A - - - - - - - - - - B

Side Panel Border, Top and Bottom
Cut 4

Side Panel Border, Top and Bottom
Cut 4

Side Panel Border, Sides
Cut 4

A - - - - - - - - - - B

Photocopy at 100%

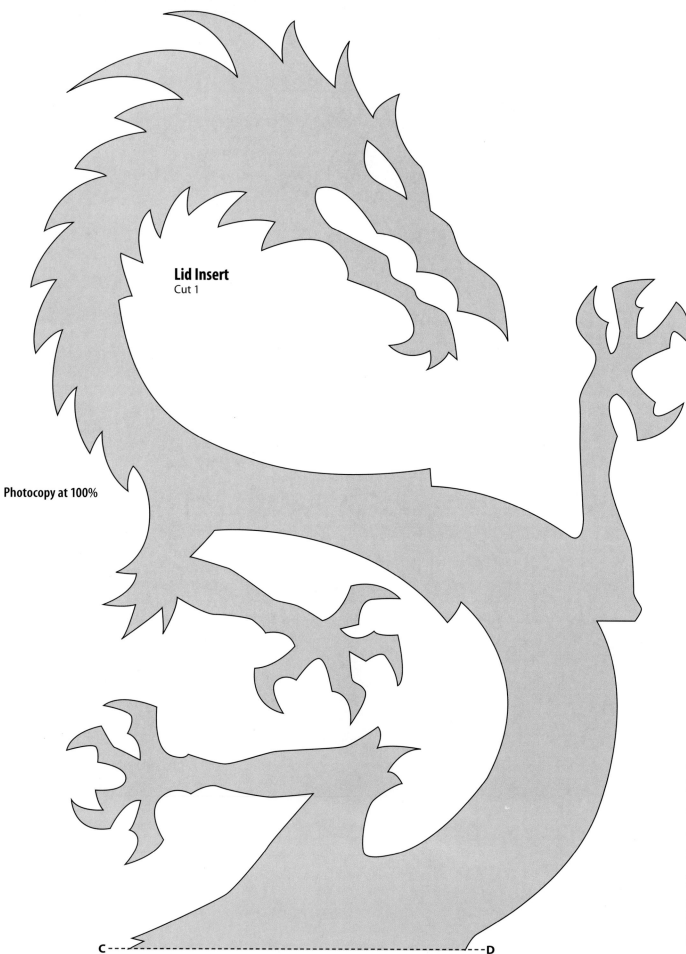

Lid Insert
Cut 1

Photocopy at 100%

C ----------------------------------- D

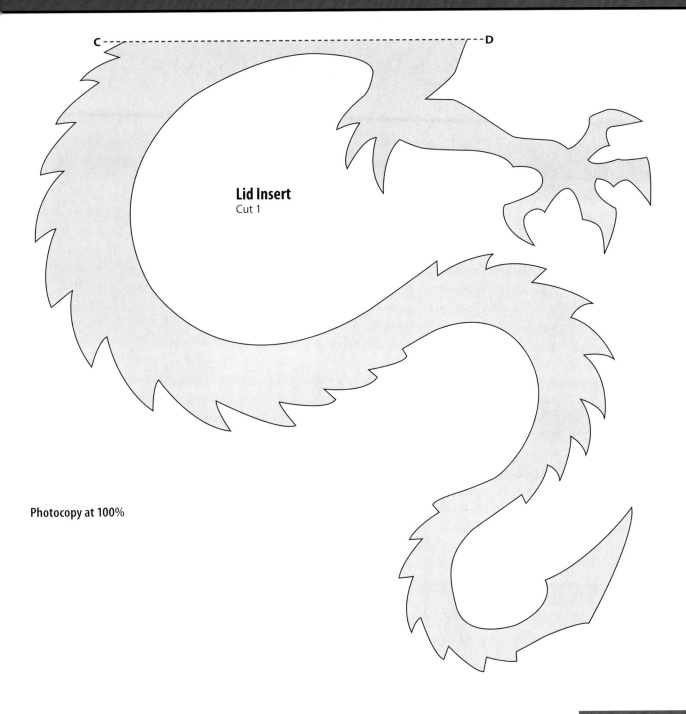

C --- D

Lid Insert
Cut 1

Photocopy at 100%

Materials:

- 4 pieces ¾" x 2" x 8' poplar (box frames)
- 4 pieces ¼" x 6" x 7" poplar (end panels, end panel designs)
- 4 pieces ¼" x 6" x 16" poplar (side panels, side panel designs)
- ¾" x 2" x 8' molding of choice (lid frame)
- ¾" x 2" x 8' poplar (lid frame, underside)
- ¾" x 9" x 18" poplar (lid panel)
- ½" x 1" x 8' poplar (bottom lid guide)
- 2 pieces ¼" x 6" x 7" padauk (end panels)
- 2 pieces ¼" x 6" x 16" padauk (side panels)
- ¼" x 9" x 18" padauk (top panel)
- ¼" x 9" x 18" poplar (bottom)

- 4 pieces ¼" x 2" x 20" poplar (side panel border, top and bottom)
- 4 pieces ¼" x 2" x 11" poplar (end panel border, top and bottom)
- 4 pieces ¼" x 2" x 10" poplar (end panel border, sides)
- 4 pieces ¼" x 2¼" x 10" poplar (side panel border, sides)
- ¼" x 9" x 18" poplar (lid dragon design)
- 4 pieces 1½" x 3½" x 3½" pine (feet)
- Wood biscuits
- Assorted grits of sandpaper up to 220 grit
- Black India ink

- Clear spray lacquer, high-gloss and satin
- Masking tape
- Wood glue and two-part epoxy

Tools:

- #3 reverse-tooth blades or blades of choice
- Miter saw and table saw
- Router with ½" radius rabbet bit and decorative edge bit of choice
- Biscuit jointer or biscuit-joint router bit
- Assorted clamps

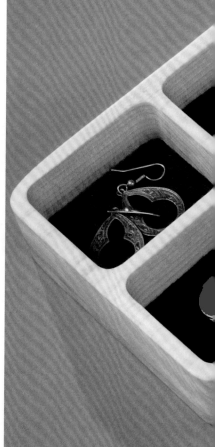

Layered Boxes

Layered boxes involve cutting multiple layers and gluing them together to create a box. This technique can create many unique shapes and often gives you the opportunity to incorporate contrasting woods and inlays into a project.

Maple Leaf Jewelry Box,
by Gary MacKay, page 83.

Texas Hold-'Em Caddie

This handy storage box is cut in layers making it easy to adjust the size to your needs.

By Gary MacKay

Decorated with the suits from a deck of cards, this stylish box stows everything but the pretzels!

Whether you're hosting poker night or meeting at your friend's house, this handsome box will keep your cards and chips ready at a moment's notice. The design is simple to scroll and can easily be modified to accommodate enough chips for any size group. This handcrafted poker caddie makes an ideal gift—stock it with a new deck of cards and some inexpensive chips for your favorite player.

In designing this box, my first consideration was to have the drawers hold two standard decks of playing cards and 100 standard-size poker chips. In order to cut the project with a scroll saw, a box this size needs to be made by laminating wood together. The box is made from one piece of ¾" by 5½" by 48" wood with a ¼"-thick front and back lamination added for contrast.

If you need to store more chips, add more layers.

Materials & Tools

Materials:
- ¾" x 5½" x 48" poplar or wood of choice (for box and drawers)
- ½" x 5½" x 8" poplar or wood of choice (for drawer sections and drawer pulls)
- ¼" x 5½" x 24" walnut or wood of choice (for box and drawer fronts and backs)
- Temporary bond spray adhesive
- Double-sided tape
- Sandpaper, assorted grits
- Wood glue
- Clear packaging tape
- Clear finish of choice

Tools:
- #5 and #7 reverse-tooth blades or blades of choice
- Drill with ¹⁄₁₆"-diameter twist drill bit
- 6 screw-type bar clamps with 6" capacity
- 10 scrap wood clamping blocks (¾" x 1½" x 6")
- Belt sander (optional)
- 1"- or 1½"-diameter drum sander
- Flat-bladed screwdriver
- Detail sander (optional)

TIP STAYING ON THE LINE

Go slowly when cutting corners with the scroll saw table tilted as the blade has a tendency to climb away from the pattern line.

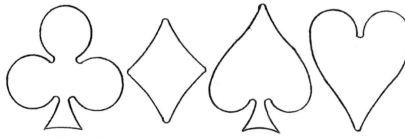

Four Suit Drawer Pulls

Photocopy at 100%

Cutting the Box

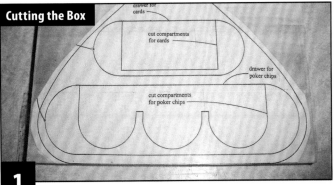

1 Prepare the wood and patterns. Make nine photocopies of the pattern. Use a #7 blade to cut the ¾" x 5½" x 48" piece of poplar into six 8"-long pieces. Apply spray adhesive to the back of the patterns and line up the straight bottom pattern line with the finished edge of the wood. Cover the patterns with clear packaging tape. Drill two ¹⁄₁₆"-diameter blade entry holes where indicated on the pattern for each of the six pieces.

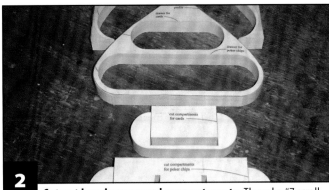

2 Cut out box drawers and compartments. Thread a #7 scroll saw blade through the ¹⁄₁₆"-diameter blade entry holes. Then, cut out the drawer for the cards and the drawer for the poker chips. Cut out the compartment for the cards and the compartments for the poker chips from the drawer pieces you removed from the main blank. Cut the outside profile of the box. Complete the cut outs for all six pieces. (**Note:** Set one drawer for cards and one drawer for poker chips aside. You will replace them with ½"-thick drawers sections in Step 5).

Assembling the Layers

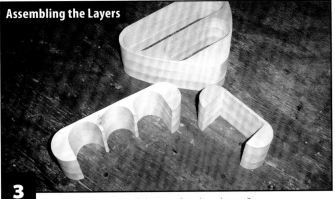

3 Glue up the box and drawer laminations. Remove any wood fuzzies, using 220-grit sandpaper. Glue up three sections of the box, three sections of the chip drawer, and three sections of the card drawer. Apply a thin layer of wood glue between each piece and stack the pieces together, being sure to line everything up.

4 Clamp three sections of the box and drawers together. Use three clamps and six scrap wood blocks to clamp the box sections together. Wait 5 minutes, then unclamp the pieces, clean up any glue squeeze-out, and re-clamp. Use two clamps and two scrap wood blocks to clamp the poker chips drawer sections together. Use one clamp and two scrap wood blocks to clamp the card drawer sections together. Follow the same procedure to clean up any glue squeeze-outs for the two drawers. Let the glue dry overnight.

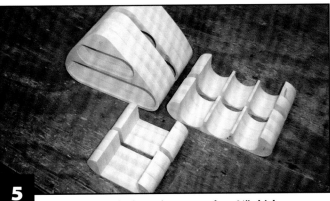

5 Cut out the ½"-thick sections to replace ¾"-thick sections. Use spray adhesive to attach patterns for the card drawer and the chip drawer to the ½" x 5½" x 8" piece of poplar for drawer laminations. Cover the blank with clear packaging tape, and cut out the two drawers and compartments. Repeat Steps 3 and 4, using your ½"-thick sections to replace one ¾"-thick section in the drawers.

6 Sand and glue-up the box and compartments. Use a 1" - or 1½"-diameter drum sander to smooth the drawer openings and poker chip compartments. Use a detail sander or sandpaper with a wooden block to smooth the inside of the card compartment. Glue-up the remaining box and drawer pieces. Clamp as before, and clean up any glue squeeze-out. Let the glued-up pieces dry overnight.

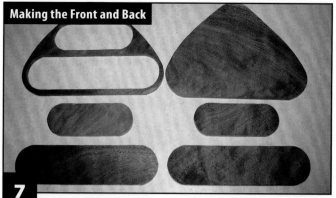

Making the Front and Back

7

Prepare the front and back pieces for the box and the drawers. Use the drum sander and the detail sander or sandpaper to smooth the areas where the box and compartments were glued together. Using a #5 scroll saw blade, or your blade of choice, cut the walnut into three 8"-long pieces. Use several strips of double-sided tape to attach two 8"-long pieces together. Use spray adhesive to adhere a pattern to the top piece of your stacked pieces of wood. Cover with clear tape. Drill the two ¹/₁₆"-diameter blade entry holes where indicated on the pattern. Cut out the two drawers—do not cut out the compartments—and cut the outside profile of the box. Use spray adhesive to adhere a pattern to the last 8" piece of wood, and apply clear tape as before. Cut only the outside profile—this will become the back of the box. Separate the two pieces using the flat-bladed screwdriver. Glue and clamp the front and back pieces to the box. Glue and clamp the front and back drawer pieces to the drawers.

8

Glue on drawer pulls and finish the card caddie. Use the drum sander to smooth out the drawer openings. Use the belt sander and sandpaper to smooth the drawers and outside box profile. Tilt the right side of the scroll saw table down 5°. Adhere the patterns for the drawer pulls to the remaining piece of ½"-thick poplar, and cut out the pulls in a counter-clockwise direction. Glue the diamond-shaped drawer pull centered onto the card drawer and glue the three other drawer pulls onto the poker chip drawer. Allow the glue to dry overnight. Apply your clear finish of choice. Be sure to set your saw table back to a 90°-angle.

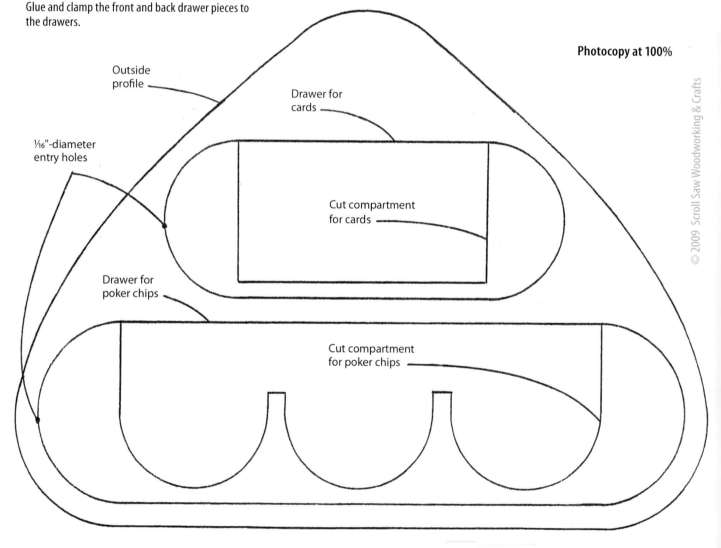

Photocopy at 100%

Outside profile

Drawer for cards

¹/₁₆"-diameter entry holes

Cut compartment for cards

Drawer for poker chips

Cut compartment for poker chips

Nesting Basket Trio

Cut, assemble, and finish these layered baskets in a single day

By Dave Van Ess

A set of nesting baskets makes a delightful handmade gift.

These layered baskets are very easy to make. Once you're familiar with the simple techniques, you'll be surprised at how quickly you can create a set. In fact, when people ask me if I made them myself, my standard reply is, "They were lumber this morning!"

All you need to get started is a piece of ¾" x 8½" x 25" hardwood. Walnut and cherry are good choices. For a completely different look, use pine and color the wood with egg dye to make Easter baskets.

By using cyanoacrylate (CA) glue, CA glue accelerator, and an oil finish, it's easy to finish the baskets in one day. Wood glue or a different finish will increase the drying time.

ASSEMBLY CHART: Follow the chart below and the labels on the pattern to assemble the bowls. The bowls are designed to neatly nest inside each other for storage when not in use.

Basket	Top Ring	Second Ring	Third Ring	Fourth Ring
A	#1	#2	#3	#4
B	#1	#2	#3	#4
C	#2	#3	#4	NA

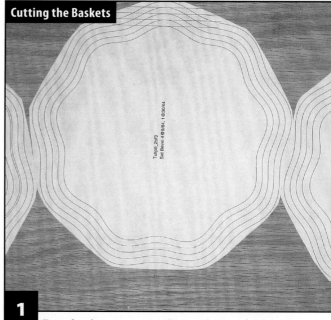

Cutting the Baskets

1 **Transfer the patterns to the wood.** Choose a piece of wood that is clear of knots. Apply spray adhesive to the back of the patterns and position them onto the blank. Align the straight entry lines on the patterns with the grain. This helps hide the joints when the rings are glued back together. Apply clear packaging tape on top of the patterns as a blade lubricant to reduce burning when cutting dense hardwoods.

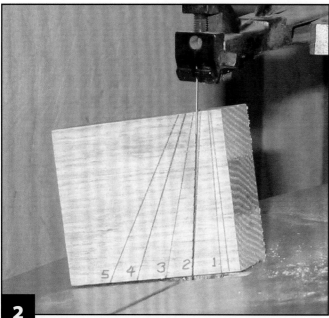

2 **Create an angle block.** Use scraps from the corner of your stock to glue up a 3" x 3" block of wood. Measure in ¼" from the edge and use a ruler to make a mark perpendicular to the stock. Measure in and make a mark at ³⁄₁₆", ⁹⁄₁₆", ¹⁵⁄₁₆", 1⁵⁄₁₆", and 1¹¹⁄₁₆". Draw a line from the top of the first line to each of these marks to create a series of angled lines. Number the lines from 1 to 5. Cut off the top of the block so it will fit under the saw arm.

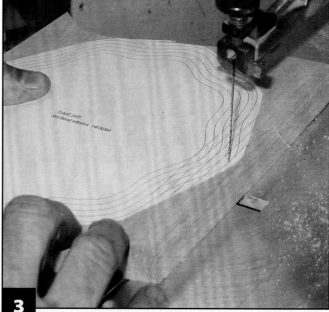

3 **Cut the rings.** Use the angle block to set the saw table to Angle 1. Cut in along the entry line and make three cuts on Pattern 1 to make two rings. Make four cuts at Angle 2 on Pattern 2 to produce three rings. Make four cuts at Angle 3 on Pattern 3. Make four more cuts at Angle 4 on Pattern 1. Set the saw to cut at Angle 5 and cut the three bases. This will give you 11 rings and three bases. Label the parts before removing the patterns.

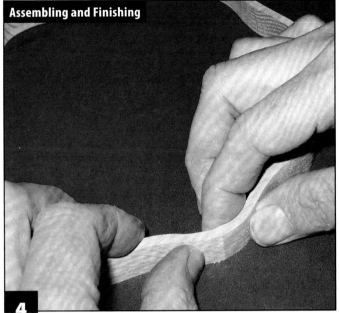

4 **Glue the rings back together.** To avoid blade entry holes, the rings are cut with the grain. Use a medium thickness cyanoacrylate (CA) glue to glue the rings back together. The glue sets in about 10 seconds if you use CA accelerator to speed the drying time. These rings will need some sanding to smooth the glue joint. Little imperfections in the cutting or slight burn marks make the finished product look more like a real basket.

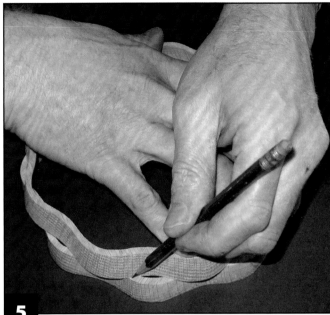

5 **Stack and glue the rings together.** Sort the rings into three piles based on the chart. Place the top ring face down on the work surface. Place Ring 2 on top of Ring 1 and mark the spots where Ring 2 intersects Ring 1. Set Ring 2 aside, add a few drops of thick, gap-filling CA glue to the intersection points on Ring 1 and reposition Ring 2 on top of Ring 1. Press Ring 2 in place until the glue dries. Use the same techniques to attach the remaining rings and the bases.

6 **Apply the finish.** These baskets are meant to be touched. Since fingers are oily, I suggest an oil finish. If these baskets are to be used with food, use a food-safe finish. Apply the oil to the baskets, wait a few minutes, then wipe off any excess. If the baskets are not going to be handled, then lacquer or varnish is an acceptable finish. The baskets can also be left unfinished and allowed to develop a natural patina with age.

Materials & Tools

Materials:
- ¾" x 8½" x 25" wood of choice
- Temporary bond spray adhesive
- Medium-thickness cyanoacrylate (CA) glue
- Thick, gap-filling CA glue
- Accelerator for CA glue
- Tung oil or finish of choice
- Sandpaper, assorted grits

Tools:
- #9 precision ground skip-tooth blades or blades of choice
- Clamps or weights (to hold layers in place when gluing, optional)

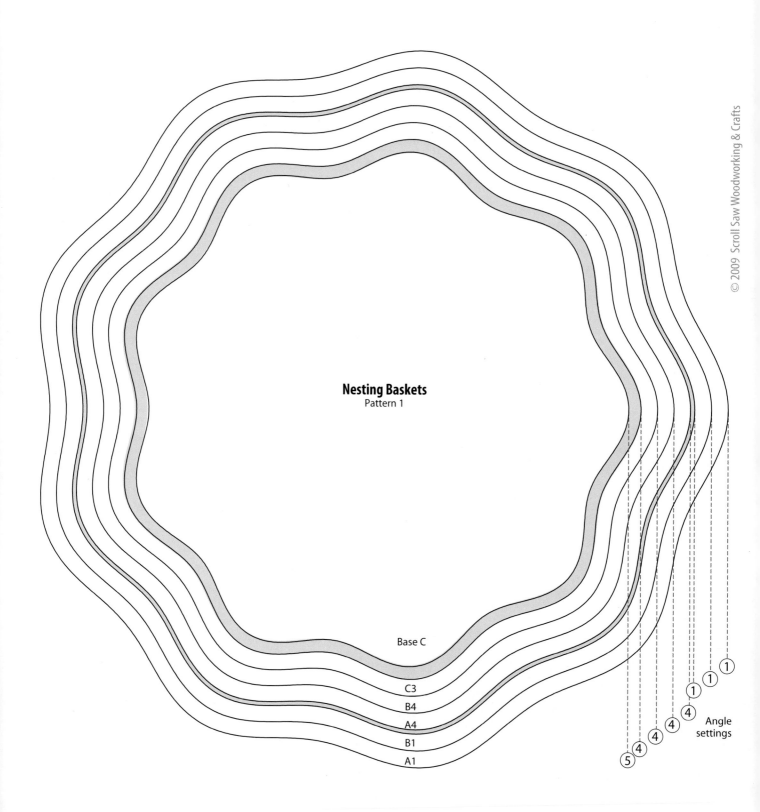

Nesting Baskets
Pattern 1

Base C

C3

B4

A4

B1

A1

Angle
settings

① ① ① ④ ④ ④ ④ ⑤

Photocopy at 110%

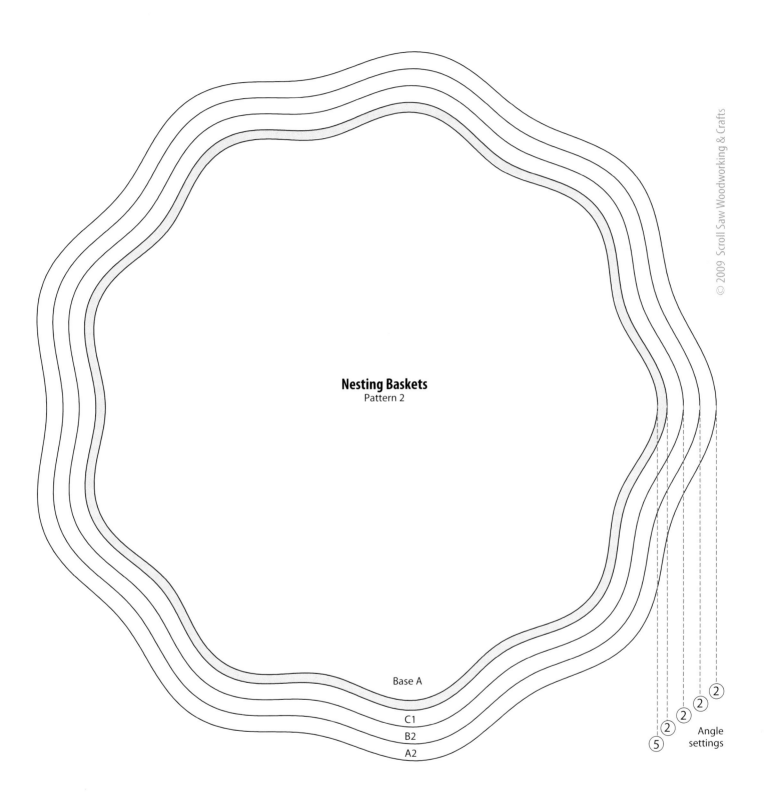

Nesting Baskets
Pattern 2

Base A

C1

B2

A2

Angle
settings

⑤ ② ② ② ②

© 2009 Scroll Saw Woodworking & Crafts

Photocopy at 110%

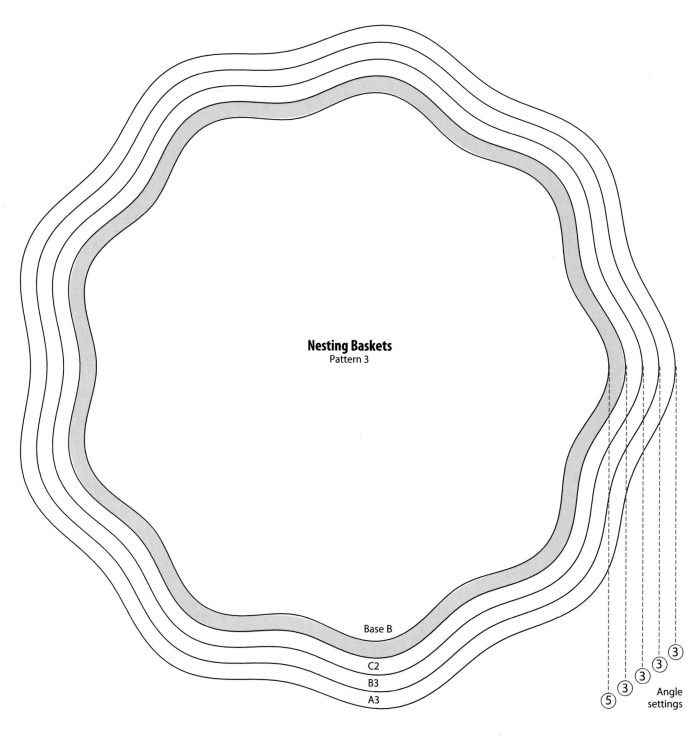

Nesting Baskets
Pattern 3

Base B

C2

B3

A3

⑤ ③ ③ ③ ③

Angle
settings

Photocopy at 110%

Maple Leaf Jewelry Box

Inlay contrasting woods for a striking presentation

By Gary MacKay

With a choice of 12 different patterns to embellish the box sides, you can easily create your own unique jewelry box. I've chosen a simple maple leaf design to inlay in the lid, but you could use a variety of designs to personalize your box.

Testing Table Angles for Inlay Work

Use several strips of double-sided tape to stack two pieces of scrap together and transfer the test pattern to the blank. Some scrollers do not recommend using double-sided tape for inlay work; however, I have not found it to be troublesome. Use the same size stock and same blade that you will use for your inlay project. Drill four 1/16"-diameter holes where indicated on the pattern. Tilt the right side of your scroll saw table down 3°. Cut out one of the pattern segments in a counterclockwise direction. The bottom piece should drop out, and the top piece should fit snugly into the hole in the bottom blank. If the top piece is too tight to fit into the bottom piece, decrease the tilt of the table. If it fits loosely into the bottom piece, increase the tilt of the table, and make another test cut.

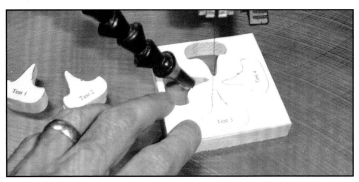

Creating the Box Sides and Base

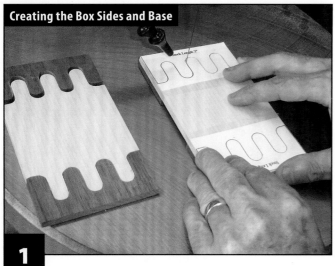

1 Construct the box sides. Cut the box sides to the dimensions listed in the materials list. Attach contrasting stock to each end for stack cutting. Transfer the corner pattern of your choice and cut using a #2/0 blade. Dry fit the pieces together before gluing them in place. Wipe up excess glue with a rag. Allow them to dry overnight.

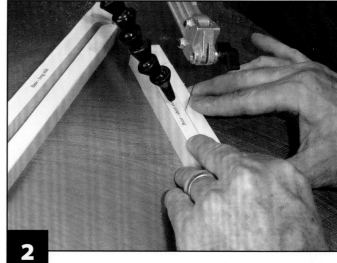

2 Cut the box base and lid slot. Use spray adhesive to attach the patterns and cut two long and two short base sides using a #5 reverse-tooth blade. Use spray adhesive to adhere the lid knob slot pattern to one of the long box sides. Use a #2/0 blade to cut out the lid knob slot.

3 Cut 45° miters on each end of the base sides and box sides. They can be cut by tilting the scroll saw table to 45° or on a table saw. Place the base sides, mitered side down, against a straight edge, alternating long and short pieces. Apply masking tape over each corner joint and halfway over one open end. Turn the taped pieces over and apply wood glue to all the miters. Roll up the base sides, using the masking tape to join the final two sides. Place the base against a 90° square. Clean up any glue squeeze-out, and let dry overnight. Repeat the process for the box sides.

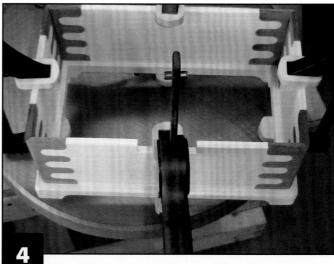

4 Glue the box sides onto the base. Remove the masking tape from the base and the box sides. Sand off any dried glue, and round over the corners. Apply wood glue to the bottom of the box sides. Place the box sides on the base, centering the sides onto the base. You should be able to see ¼" of wood on the outside and inside of the base. Clamp the box sides onto the base. Clean up any glue squeeze-out, and let the glue dry. Measure the inside box length and width. Transfer your measurements and cut out the box bottom, using a #5 reverse-tooth blade. Glue the bottom in place.

With multiple corner designs to choose from, you can create a variety of custom jewelry boxes.

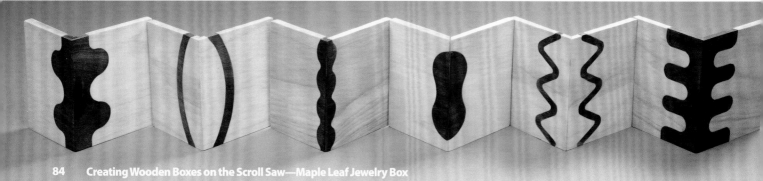

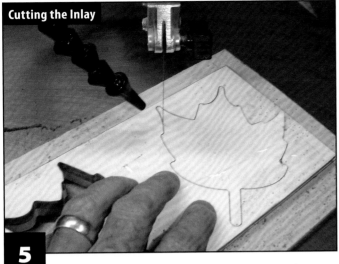

Cutting the Inlay

5 **Cut the maple leaf inlays.** Cut the lid blanks to size. Center the leaf inlay stock on the lid blank and attach them together with thin double-sided tape. Transfer the inlay pattern to the blank. Drill two ¹⁄₁₆"-diameter blade entry holes where indicated on the pattern. With your saw table tilted, (see Testing Table Angles for Inlay Work) cut out both maple leaf inlays with a #5 reverse-tooth blade. A larger blade is recommended because it is more easily bowed with the table tilted, but the tilt will compensate for the larger kerf. Separate the pieces and use cotton swabs to spread glue onto the edges of the maple leaves. Glue the leaves into the lid stock.

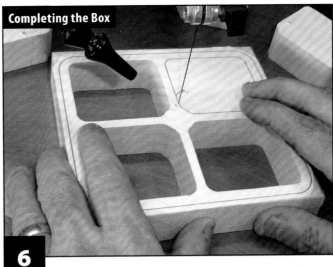

Completing the Box

6 **Assemble the lid and lift-out tray.** Make sure your table is square to your blade. Apply a layer of wood glue to both the back surface of the lid with the inlays and the other lid piece. Clamp the two pieces together and let dry. Transfer the lift-out tray pattern to the stock. Drill four ¹⁄₈"-diameter blade entry holes where indicated on the pattern. Use a #9 reverse-tooth blade to cut out the compartments. Save one of the cut out waste pieces if you plan to line your compartments. Leave the pattern on the tray, and glue the tray bottom in place. After the glue dries, use a #9 reverse-tooth blade to cut the outside profile of the tray.

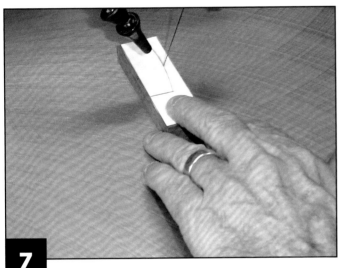

7 **Cut out the lid knob.** Transfer the pattern to the stock. Use a #5 reverse-tooth blade to make the side cuts. Back the blade out from the cut. Tilt the left side of the table down 10°, and cut the curved portion of the knob. Return the saw table to 90°. Find the center of the lid side, and glue the lid knob in place so it lines up with the lid slot cut in the box side.

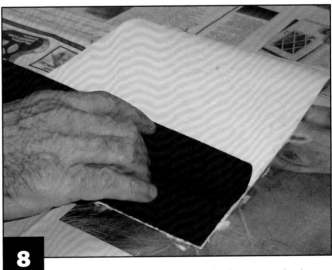

8 **Finish the inside of the box.** Transfer the patterns for the dividers to the stock and cut them out with a #5 reverse-tooth blade. Glue the felt to a piece of poster board with wood glue. Line the bottom of the box. Use one of the scraps from the compartments as a pattern, and cut out felt squares to line the compartment sections.

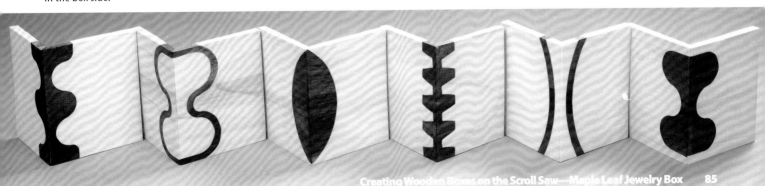

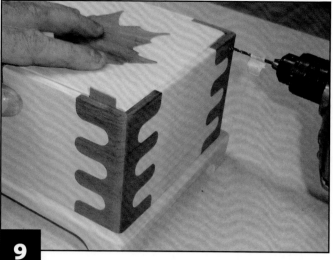

9 **Fit the lid to the box.** Measure the distance of your box from the box bottom to the bottom of the lid knob slot. Make two lid stops based on this measurement and glue the stops in the inside front corners. Test to ensure that a ³⁄₃₂"-diameter drill bit provides a tight fit for your finishing nail. Fit the lid in place, and drill 1"-deep holes on both sides through the box sides and lid, ½" in from the back of the box and ¼" down from the top of the box. If the lid interferes with the back of the box when opening, round over the back edge of the lid with your sander until it opens smoothly.

10 **Complete the box.** Sand the dividers, tray, lid, and box. Apply your finish before attaching the lid. Use your finish of choice. I use boiled linseed oil, followed by one or two coats of clear shellac, and then a good paste wax. When dry, fit the lid by inserting both nails all the way into the holes. Mark the nails at the point where they meet the box sides with masking tape. Use a hacksaw or Dremel cutting tool to cut the nails about ¹⁄₁₆" short of the masking tape. Both nails should be recessed inside the holes. Fill the holes with wood filler.

Materials:

- 2 pieces ¼" x 3½" x 10" poplar (box sides)
- 2 pieces ¼" x 3½" x 6" poplar (box sides)
- 8 pieces ¼" x 3½" x 2" walnut or contrasting stock (wood joints, some require only 1" wide pieces)
- 2 pieces ¾" x 1" x 10½" poplar (base long sides)
- 2 pieces ¾" x 1" x 6½" poplar (base short sides)
- ¼" x 5½" x 9½" plywood (box bottom, estimated dimensions)
- 2 pieces ¼" x 5¾" x 10" poplar (lid)
- ¼" x 4" x 8½" walnut (maple leaf inlays)
- 2 pieces ¼" x 3" x 3" scrap wood (test inlays)
- 1" x 5" x 5½" poplar (lift out tray, may substitute 2 pieces ½"-thick pieces)
- ¼" x 5" x 5½" poplar (tray bottom)
- ½" x 1" x 3" walnut (lid knob)
- ¼" x 1¼" x 9½" poplar (long compartment divider)
- 3 pieces ¼" x 1¼" x 5½" poplar (short compartment dividers)

Materials & Tools

- 2 pieces ½" x ½" x 2¹³⁄₁₆" poplar (lid stops, estimated lengths)
- Temporary bond spray adhesive
- Double-sided tape
- Masking tape
- Cotton swabs
- Wood glue
- Assorted grits of sandpaper
- Clear finish of choice
- Wood filler
- 2 finishing nails, 2" long
- 8½" x 11" poster board
- 8½" x 11" felt

Tools:

- #2/0, #5, and #9 reverse-tooth blades or blades of choice
- Drill with ¹⁄₁₆"-, ³⁄₃₂"-, and ⅛"-diameter drill bits
- Assorted clamps
- Large square (16" x 24")
- A palm, orbital, or belt sander
- Hacksaw or metal cutting Dremel tool (for cutting nails)

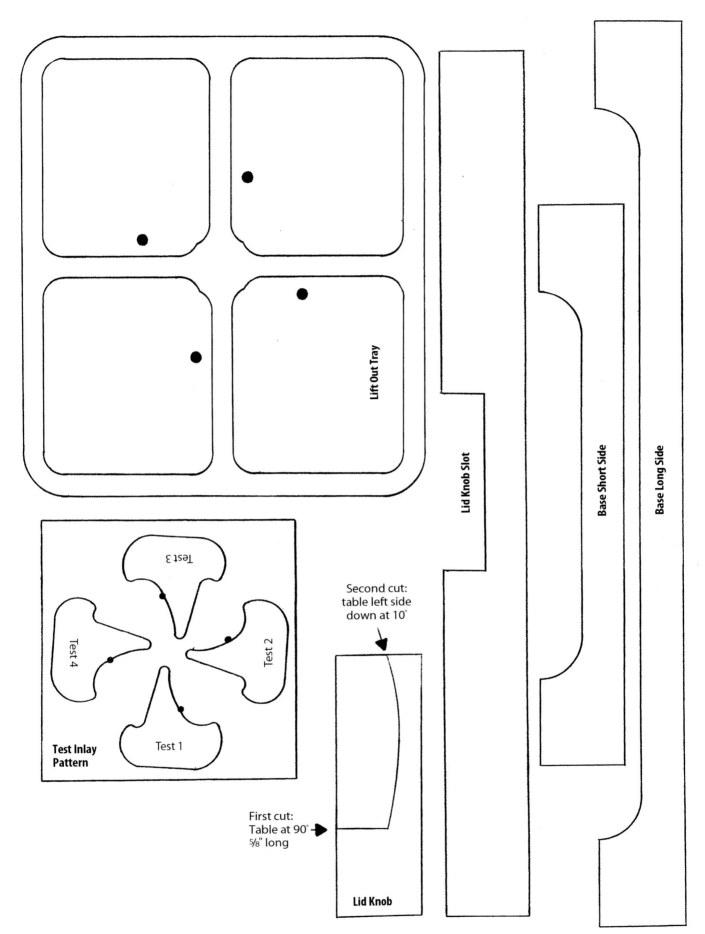

Lift Out Tray

Lid Knob Slot

Base Short Side

Base Long Side

Test 3

Test 4

Test 2

Test 1

Test Inlay Pattern

Second cut:
table left side
down at 10°

First cut:
Table at 90°
⅝" long

Lid Knob

Photocopy at 110%

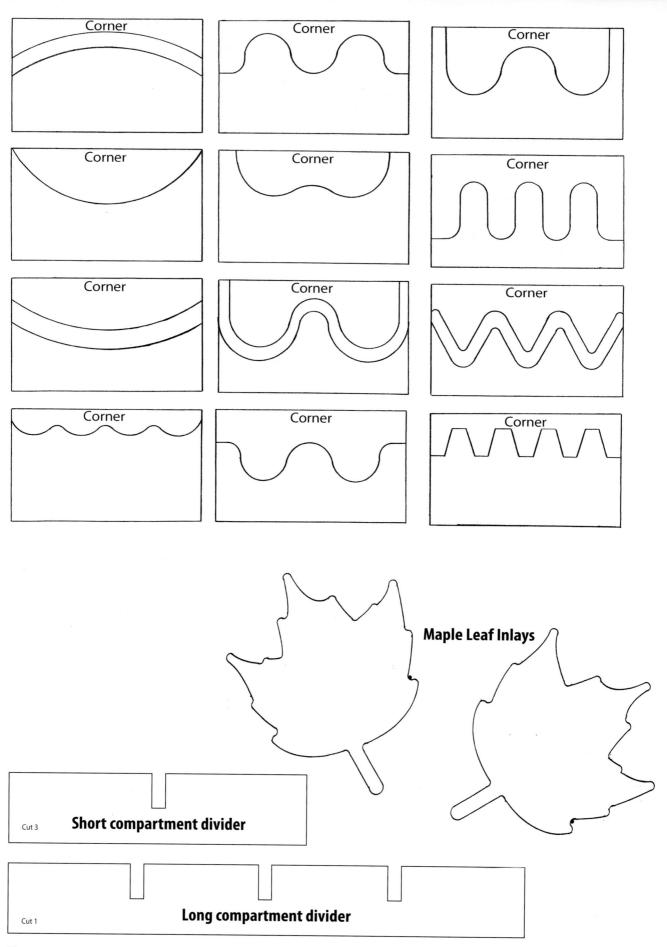

Corner

Corner

Corner

Corner

Corner

Corner

Corner

Corner

Corner

Corner

Corner

Corner

Maple Leaf Inlays

Cut 3 **Short compartment divider**

Cut 1 **Long compartment divider**

Photocopy at 170%

Four-in-One Boxes

You'll find plenty of uses for these mahogany beauties

By Joan West

Anyone can use a few extra boxes to store easy-to-lose items like keys, jewelry, or even a few favorite recipes. You'll waste very little wood doing this simple project, and you will be more than satisfied when you wind up with four attractive boxes of varying sizes.

Mahogany is my wood of choice for this project because it sands easily and its high oil content creates a beautiful luster. Other woods that work well include pine, basswood, and butternut. I do not recommend using hardwoods, such as oak, unless you are prepared to spend a great deal of time on the sanding process.

Step 1: Prepare the work pieces. Make 15 copies of the pattern. Seven copies are for the wall pieces; eight copies are for the end pieces. For the end pieces, just cut on the outside lines. Prepare the mahogany by sanding both sides to 150 grit.

Spray the patterns with temporary bond spray adhesive, and attach all copies to the wood in the following manner: Place the patterns of all seven wall pieces and the eight end pieces on their respective lengths of wood. Place them along the bottom edge of the wood according to the grain direction indicated on the pattern. Refer to the Suggested Pattern Layout on page 92.

Step 2: Cut the dotted lines. Cut through the dotted line that separates the lid from the base on all wall piece patterns and all end piece patterns. A table saw is recommended to make this cut.

Step 3: Number each piece. Number each wall and lid piece so they match up in final assembly.

Step 4: Cut the wall pieces. Using a #7 blade, cut apart each wall piece for both the lid and base on all seven patterns. Accurate cutting is

important since each cutting line affects the cutting line of another box. Continue using the #7 blade to cut out each end piece.

▲ **Step 5: Test fit the boxes.** For a more uniform finish, dry assemble the large box and check how the pieces fit. To secure pieces in dry assembly stages, wipe away all dust and apply small pieces of double-sided tape and/or wrap with masking tape. You also may want to clamp to reduce chances of pieces shifting as you work. Use the edges where the lid and base meet as alignment reference points. If there are any pieces that are significantly out of fit, re-cut or sand to align. Go over all surfaces with a hand-held belt sander using 100-grit sandpaper. After sanding, remove the tape and/or clamps.

▲ **Step 6: Round the edges.** To round the edges for the large box, rout a gentle radius on the outside edges of both sides of all lid and base wall pieces excluding the bottom edge.

Step 7: Wipe away all sawdust from the lid and base pieces of all boxes. Glue together all lid and base pieces excluding end pieces, two to three sections at a time. Use a finger to apply a thin but thorough coat of glue on both surfaces. Clamp the pieces together and let dry seven to eight hours. Use at least four clamps equally spaced and tightened with even pressure.

TIP **A FEW WORDS ABOUT GLUE**

Don't use too much glue when gluing together and clamping lid and base pieces or the individual pieces may slip under pressure. Be sure to wipe the excess glue that seeps out when tightening the clamps.

▲ **Step 8: Sand the box insides.** Using a drum sander with 100-grit sandpaper, sand the insides of the boxes to achieve a uniform surface.

▲ **Step 9: Sand the base and lid.** Unless you have a flawless cutting technique, the edges where the base and lid meet will not be perfectly even. To obtain a gap-free seam between the base and the lid, place the edge flat against a stationary belt sander with 100-grit sandpaper until it is even.

Step 10: Rout the end pieces of the large box. For the large box only, rout both sides of each end piece just like you did for the wall pieces. Do not rout the bottom edge. Note that the area at the back of the boxes, where the lid and base meet (refer to pattern), should not be routed. This area needs to be flat so the hinges can be attached.

▲ **Step 11: Glue the end pieces.** Make sure the edges where the lid and base meet are perfectly aligned. Clamp and let dry.

▲ **Step 12: Sand the outsides of the boxes.** For the medium, small, and extra small boxes, sand all of the outside surfaces flush. For the large box, sand the bottom flush. A stationary belt sander with 100-grit sandpaper is the best tool for the job.

▲ **Step 13: Sand all surfaces to at least 220 grit.** A flap sander is recommended for this step.

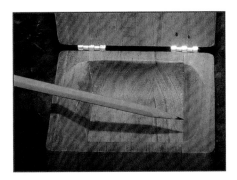

▲ **Optional step: Sand the inside edges.** For the extra small box, use a drum sander with 100-grit sandpaper to sand the inside edges of the end pieces to provide more room inside the box.

Step 14: Attach the hinges to the lid and base. Predrill, using a bit one size smaller than the screw, to eliminate the possibility of splitting the wood. Place the hinges approximately ¼" to ½" from the side edges.

Step 15: Finish. Do any touch-up sanding at this point. Apply one coat of Danish oil to all surfaces of each box, following the manufacturer's directions. Make sure the oil is completely dry. This may take up to two days depending on humidity. Then, apply paste wax and buff.

Materials & Tools

Materials:

- 1 piece, ⅞" x 54" x 6" mahogany (seven wall pieces for all four boxes)
- 1 piece, ⅞" x 15" x 6" mahogany (two large box end pieces)
- 1 piece, ⅞" x 13" x 5" mahogany (two medium box end pieces)
- 1 piece, ⅞" x 11" x 4" mahogany (two small box end pieces)
- 1 piece, ⅞" x 9" x 3" mahogany (two extra small box end pieces)
- Double-sided tape and/or masking tape
- Wood glue
- Temporary bond spray adhesive
- 8 solid brass hinges, ¾" x ¹¹⁄₁₆"
- Danish oil, natural
- Paste wax
- Sandpaper, 100, 150, and 220 grits

Tools:

- #7 precision ground tooth blades
- Small drill bits for predrilling hinges
- Router with ⅜"-radius bit
- Bar-style clamps
- Flap sander (recommended)
- Drum sander
- Stationary belt sander
- Hand-held belt sander
- Table saw (recommended)

TIP DON'T GET HUNG UP ON HINGES

When attaching hinges, place a business card at the back edge between the lid and the base to create a small space at the back. This eliminates an inevitable gap in the front edge where the lid and base meet.

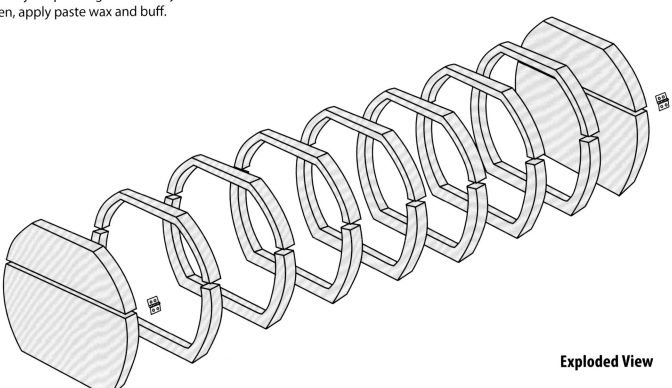

Exploded View

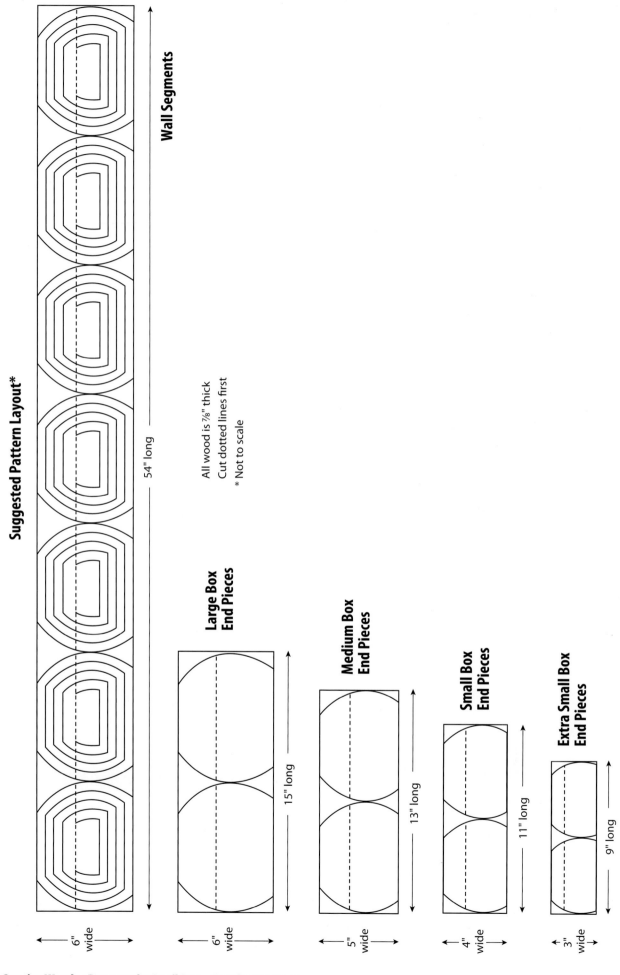

Suggested Pattern Layout*

Wall Segments

54" long

6" wide

All wood is ⅞" thick
Cut dotted lines first
* Not to scale

**Large Box
End Pieces**

15" long

6" wide

**Medium Box
End Pieces**

13" long

5" wide

**Small Box
End Pieces**

11" long

4" wide

**Extra Small Box
End Pieces**

9" long

3" wide

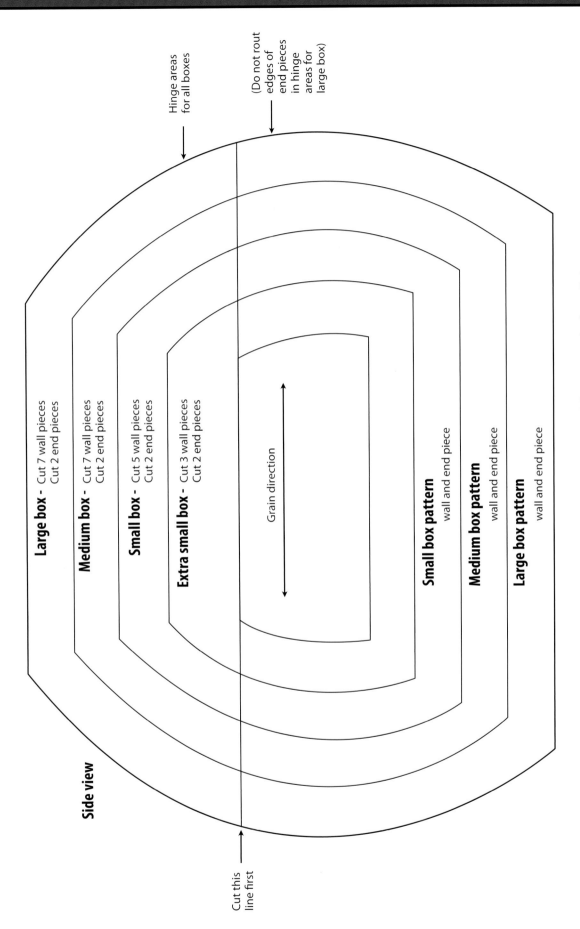

Hinge areas for all boxes

(Do not rout edges of end pieces in hinge areas for large box)

Large box - Cut 7 wall pieces
Cut 2 end pieces

Medium box - Cut 7 wall pieces
Cut 2 end pieces

Small box - Cut 5 wall pieces
Cut 2 end pieces

Extra small box - Cut 3 wall pieces
Cut 2 end pieces

Grain direction

Small box pattern
wall and end piece

Medium box pattern
wall and end piece

Large box pattern
wall and end piece

Make seven copies for wall pieces
Make eight copies for end pieces

Side view

Cut this line first

Photocopy at 100%

© 2009 Scroll Saw Woodworking & Crafts

Patriotic Flag Box

An attractive inside display for Old Glory

By Joan West

Honor those who sacrifice their lives for our freedom and proclaim your loyalty to your country with this flag display box. The project includes wood, brass, and Plexiglas. Though Flag Day is not traditionally a gift-giving holiday, this year you may want to make this attractive box for a serviceman that you know or a serviceman's family.

TIP **SUPER DUST CONTROL**

For dust control when sanding the box wall, clamp the hose of a shop-vacuum to the working surface.

Step 1: Gather and prepare your materials. Wearing a dust mask, sand all wood with 220-grit sandpaper. Next, make five copies of the box wall pattern and apply the pattern to each layer of the wall with temporary bond spray adhesive. (You can stack cut the thin layers at the same time for increased accuracy.)

Step 2: Cut out each layer. Use a #7 precision ground tooth blade. Be sure to cut accurately. The more accurate your cuts now, the less time you'll spend finish sanding later.

Step 3: Glue the layers together in the order indicated on the pattern. I highly recommend gluing one layer at a time. (See Gluing with Clamps.) Let the pieces dry eight to ten hours.

Step 4: Cut the lid and base. Apply the lid and base patterns and cut them out with a #7 precision ground tooth blade.

Step 5: Cut out the Plexiglas insert. A pattern for the Plexiglas is provided. However, a more accurate pattern may be obtained by using the cutout opening of the box lid you have cut and adding ⅛" to 3⁄16" all around the edges. Wrap the Plexiglas in two layers of duct tape. Doing so lubricates the #5 Plexiglas blade so the plastic does not heat up and fuse back together behind the blade.

Step 6: Rout the edges. Using a ¼" round-over router bit, rout the top outside edges of the lid and base. Sand the lid and base surfaces with 320-grit sandpaper. Using a progression of 150- to 220-grit sandpaper, sand the inside cutout of the lid enough to soften the edge.

▲ **Step 7: On the underside of the lid, rout a rabbet for the Plexiglas.** It should be ¼" deep and 3⁄16" to ⅛" wide. Using a utility knife, carve out the areas the router can't reach.

Step 8: Sand the inside and outside surfaces of the box wall. Use a belt sander, finishing sander, and/or a drum sander. Begin with 100-grit sandpaper and work to 320 grit (The inside needs only to be worked to 150 grit).

Step 9: Glue the box wall. Center the box wall on the underside of the box lid, glue, and clamp in place. Let it dry eight to ten hours.

Step 10: Drill 5⁄8" clearance holes on the box base as indicated on the pattern. Using these holes as reference, drill ½" screw holes in the box wall. Countersink the holes on the base so the screw heads are flush.

Step 11: Attach the letters. Cut out the personalized lettering with a #2 precision ground tooth blade. Glue the letters in place.

Step 12: Cut the brass eagle. Affix the brass on top of scrap wood with two layers of clear packaging tape. Apply the eagle pattern. Spray a #2 metal-cutting blade with silicon. (I spray the blade while it's in the saw.) Cut out the eagle.

Step 13: Apply one coat of Danish oil. Carefully follow the directions on the can. Let dry 72 hours.

Step 14: Apply a satin finish coat.

▲ **Step 15: Add the Plexiglas.** Bead a thin line of caulk in the rabbet and insert the Plexiglas.

▲ **Step 16: Attach the eagle.** Carefully sand away the finish beneath the eagle mounting area and glue the eagle in place with cyanoacrylate glue. Apply weight to keep it in place and let the glue dry for an hour.

Assembly drawing

⅜" x 13⅝" x 24" chinkapin

½" screw ¾" long

⅝" hole countersunk on back

¾" x 12⅝" x 23³⁄₁₆" walnut

¾" x 12⅝" x 23³⁄₁₆" mahogany

⅛" x 10" x 18³⁄₁₆" clear acrylic glued to back face of lid

Sand slight round-over on front edge

Back

Rout ¼" round-over on front edge

Lid

Sgt Gary Browning

US Marine Corps

US Marine Corps

Center wall

1½" x 12⅝" x 23³⁄₁₆" chinkapin

¾" x 12⅝" x 23³⁄₁₆" mahogany

50 mils brass

⅜" x 13⅝" x 24" chinkapin

⅜" walnut

Materials & Tools

Materials:
- 2 pieces, ⅜" x 26" x 14" chinkapin or yellowheart (base and lid)
- 2 pieces, ¹¹⁄₁₆" x 24" x 13" mahogany (layers 1 and 5 of center)
- 2 pieces, ³⁄₁₆" x 24" x 13" walnut (layers 2 and 4 of center)
- 1½" x 24" x 13" chinkapin or yellowheart (layer 3 of center)
  The previous woods can be any combination of thicknesses as long as they equal 3¼".
- ³⁄₁₆" x 1" x 18" walnut (lettering)
- ¼" x 18¼" x 10" Plexiglas

- 50 mils x 2½" x 2½" prepolished soft brass (door kick plate available from most hardware stores or home centers)
- ⅛" x ½" screws (3)
- ⅛" x 2½" x 2½" scrap board
- Wood glue
- Danish oil
- Satin spray polyurethane
- Sandpaper, 100, 150, 220, and 320 grit
- Temporary bond spray adhesive
- Silicon spray

- Duct tape
- Clear packaging tape
- Clear caulk
- Cyanoacrylate glue

Tools:
- Router with ¼" round-over bit
- #2 metal-cutting blade
- #2 and #7 precision ground tooth blades
- #5 Plexiglas blade
- Finishing sander with 100-, 150-, 220-, and 320-grit sandpaper

- Belt sander with 100-and 150-grit sandpaper
- Oscillating sander or drum sander attachment for a drill press with 1" to 3" drums with 100-grit sandpaper
- Drill with ½"-diameter bit for screw holes in box wall, ⅝"-diameter bit for clearance holes
- Quick-grip clamps or bar-style clamps
- Utility knife
- Dust mask

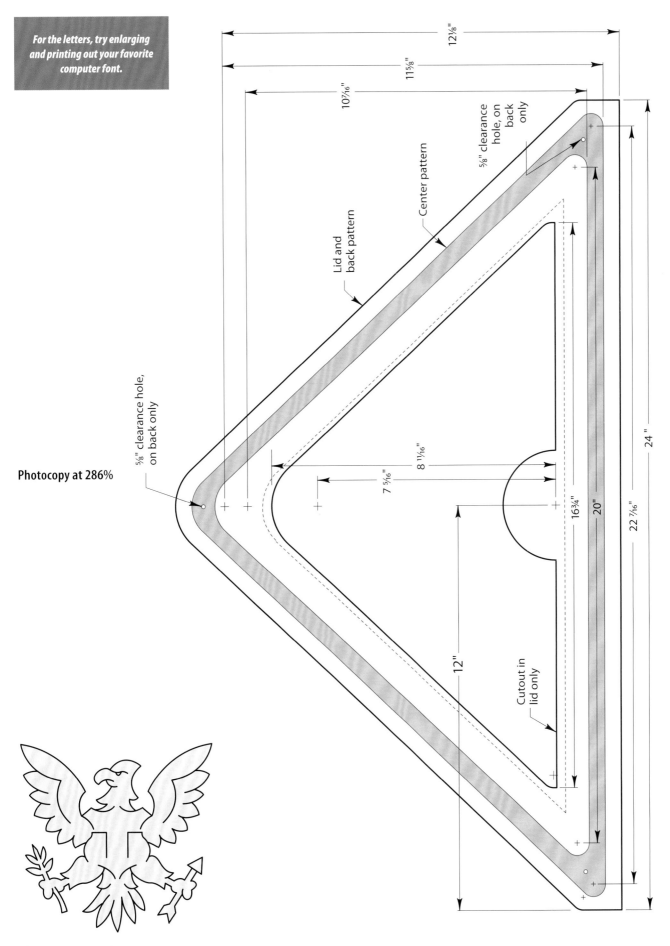

For the letters, try enlarging and printing out your favorite computer font.

12 1/8"

11 5/8"

10 7/16"

5/8" clearance hole, on back only

Center pattern

Lid and back pattern

Photocopy at 286%

5/8" clearance hole, on back only

8 11/16"

7 5/16"

16 3/4"

20"

24"

22 7/16"

12"

Cutout in lid only

Photocopy at 100%

One-of-a-Kind Boxes

As you'll see in this section, boxes aren't limited to just traditional boxes. Puzzle boxes, which can make great gifts, are some of the more unique box types. We've also included here a box with a wooden bow, a natural edge box, and a patina flower box, just to get your imagination going.

Secret Chamber Puzzle Box, by Karl Taylor, page 106.

Sliding Panel Puzzle Box

Unlock the mystery by sliding the hidden panels

By Bruce Viney

Hardwood version cut by Ben Fink

Amaze your friends and family with this ingenious puzzle box. Follow a specific sequence of movements to unlock the panels. Once the six-step puzzle has been solved, the top panel can be removed. Each panel looks identical on the outside, making the solution more difficult than it appears.

The box consists of six sides labeled A through F. Each side consists of four layers or panels. Each outer panel connects to an inner panel with a slider that fits inside a hole cut in the box side. The inner panels create the locking mechanism for the box.

The box sides, labeled Layer 3, make up the framework of the box. To make the puzzle more difficult to solve, orient the wood grain in the same direction on all six box sides. The outer panels, labeled Layer 1, move, in turn moving the inner panels that lock the box together.

The only tricky cuts are on the inside panel of Side E, which is the removable top of the box. While a miter saw makes it easier to cut the angles on the panel, you can cut the entire project with a scroll saw. To make construction and assembly easier, the panels have been color-coded in the instructional photos, patterns, and assembly diagram.

When assembling the pieces, use small amounts of glue to prevent it from squeezing out and interfering with the movement of nearby pieces. Let the glue dry for each section before moving on to the next step.

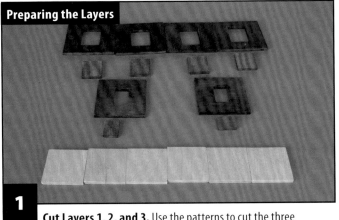

1 **Cut Layers 1, 2, and 3.** Use the patterns to cut the three different layers for each of the six sides. Label the back of each piece lightly with pencil. All six outer panels (Layer 1) are identical and can be stack cut.

2 **Dry assemble the box sides.** I built a simple jig to hold the pieces together. Screw two ¾" x 1½" pieces of wood at right angles to each other on a larger piece of wood. The raised edges make it easy to dry assemble the sides.

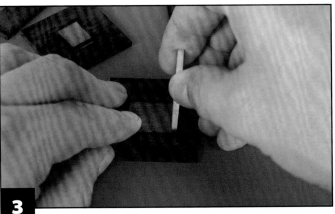

3 **Test the movement of the sliders.** Most ⅛"-thick plywood is thicker than ⅛". The sliders (Layer 2) must move the thickness of the plywood, so you may need to trim the sliders. Position each slider in its respective hole and test the open area with a piece of scrap plywood. If the slider and scrap wood do not both fit in the hole, trim the end of the slider.

4 **Cut Layer 4 of Side E.** The inside panel for the top of the box requires mitered cuts. Cut along the black lines to ensure the panel is the proper size. Tilt the right side of your saw table down at a 45° angle and cut in along the red lines. Angle the left side of your saw table down 45° and cut along the blue lines. Cut along the dotted lines with a knife to free the triangular chips.

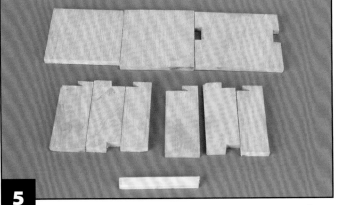

5 **Cut the remaining inner panels.** Use the patterns to cut the remaining panels for Layer 4. Layer 4 on Sides A and C are each made up of three panels. Sides B, D, and F have a single panel for Layer 4. Side E uses the panel cut in Step 4 along with a top rail. Label the back of each piece lightly with a pencil.

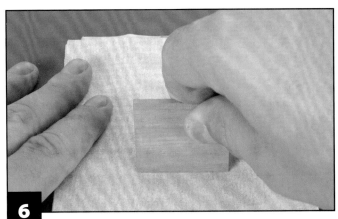

6 **Test the fit of the inner panels.** Layer 4 creates a minibox inside Layer 3. The pieces must fit snugly but move freely, especially on Sides A and C. Sand the edges of any tight panels. Sand a little from the width of each of the three panels that make up Layer 4 on Sides A and C. The panels must fit together side to side, sit flush with the sides of Layer 3, and move freely.

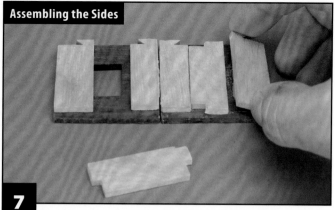

7 **Assemble Layer 4 of Sides A and C.** Begin with Side A. Position the end panels of Layer 4 on the inside face of Layer 3 so the 45° angles face left. The end panels are flush to the top and sides of Layer 3. Place the center panel in position and make sure it slides freely. Remove the center panel and glue the end panels to Layer 3. Repeat the process for Side C, but flip the panels of Layer 4 so the 45° angles face right.

8 **Finish assembling Sides A and C.** Begin with Side A. Position the center panel of Layer 4 on Layer 3 with the tab to the left and flush with the top of Layer 3. Hold the panel in place as you flip the assembly over. Glue Layer 2 through the hole in Layer 3 to Layer 4. Layer 2 is at the top of the hole in Layer 3. Glue Layer 1 to Layer 2, allowing a ¼" margin around Layer 1. Repeat the process for Side C, with the tab on Layer 4 facing to the right.

9 **Begin assembling the box.** Apply glue to the edge of Layer 3 on the right side of Assembly A and the left side of Assembly C. Glue and clamp Sides A and C to the inside of Layer 3 on Side B. The long sides of the hole in Side B should be parallel to Sides A and C. Align A and C with the edge and bottom of Side B. The top of Side B is above the tops of Sides A and C.

10 **Attach Side F to the assembly.** Glue and clamp Layer 3 of Side F to Layer 3 on Sides A, B, and C with the long sides of the hole parallel to Sides A and C. Slide Layer 1 on Sides A and C away from Side F. Dry fit Layer 4 of Side B so it rests on Layer 3 of Side F. Slide Layer 4 of Side F in to meet Layer 4 of Side B. The tabs on Layer 4 of Sides A and C align with the slots in Layer 4 of Side F.

11 **Assemble Side F.** Hold Layer 4 in position. Glue Layer 2 to Layer 4 through the hole in Layer 3. Place Layer 2 flush to the side of the hole in Layer 3 farthest from Side B. Glue and clamp Layer 1 to Layer 2. Layer 1 is centered between Sides A and C and positioned ⅛" in from the edge of Layer 3 that is farthest from Side B.

12 **Assemble Side B.** Remove Layer 4 of Side B. Slide Layer 1 of Side F toward Side B and replace Layer 4 of Side B so it rests on Layer 4 of Side F. Glue Layer 2 to Layer 4 through the hole in Layer 3. Align Layer 2 with the side of the hole farthest away from Side F. Glue and clamp Layer 1 to Layer 2. Layer 1 is centered between Sides A and C and ¼" away from the edge that is farthest from Side F.

13 **Begin assembling Side E.** Slide Layer 1 for Side F away from Side B. Slide Layer 1 of Sides A, B, and C toward Side F. Place Layer 4 of Side E in position so the angled cuts fit into the angled notches in A and C. Slide Layer 1 of Sides A, B, and C toward Side E to lock Layer 4 in place. Place Layer 3 over Layer 4 on Side E with the long sides of the hole parallel to Sides A and C. Align the edges of Layer 3 with the adjoining sides. Glue Layer 2 to Layer 4. Place Layer 2 in the side of the hole in Layer 3 farthest from Side B.

15 **Finish assembling Side E.** Glue the Top Rail in position on the inside of Layer 3, lining it up with the pencil mark made in Step 14. Clamp the Top Rail in place and allow the glue to dry. When the box is locked, you can't remove the top (Side E), but Side E will have a slight amount of play unless you install the Top Rail.

17 **Finish the puzzle box.** Brush on a light brown stain and varnish finish or apply your finish of choice. Do not let the finish interfere with the movement of the panels. Carve or woodburn designs onto Layer 1 or use printed patterns. Spray the printed patterns with artist fixative to seal the ink. Attach the printout to the wood with a light coat of wood glue. Be sure the design is symmetrical to avoid providing any clues to the puzzle's solution.

14 **Mark the position of the Top Rail.** Glue and clamp Layer 1 to Layer 2 on Side E, centering Layer 1 between Sides A and C, and allowing a ⅜" margin on the side farthest from Side B. Slide Layer 1 of Sides A, B, and C toward Side F. Slide Layer 1 of Side E toward Side B and remove Side E. With Layer 1 on Side E as far away from Side B as it will go, make a pencil mark along the edge of Layer 4 on the inside of Layer 3. Make the mark on the side farthest from Side B.

16 **Assemble Side D.** Slide Layer 1 of Sides A, B, and C away from Side F and slide Layer 1 of Side F toward Side B. Glue and clamp Layer 3 of Side D flush with the faces of Layer 3 on Sides A, C, and F. The long sides of the hole run parallel to Sides A and C. Slide Layer 4 in place so it rests on Layer 3 of Side F. Glue Layer 2 to Layer 4 through the hole in Layer 3. Align Layer 2 with the side of the hole closest to Side F. Glue and clamp Layer 1 to Layer 2, centering Layer 1 between Sides A and C and positioned ¼" away from Side E.

Using the puzzle box

To put the top on:
Step 1: Move Side D toward Side E.
Step 2: Move Side F toward Side D.
Step 3: Move Sides A, B, and C down toward Side F.
Step 4: Slide Side E away from the Top Rail and set Side E in place with the Top Rail toward Side D.

To lock the puzzle box:
Step 1: Move Side E toward Side D.
Step 2: Move Sides A, B, and C up toward Side E.
Step 3: Move Side F toward Side B.
Step 4: Move Side D toward Side F.

Assembly Diagram

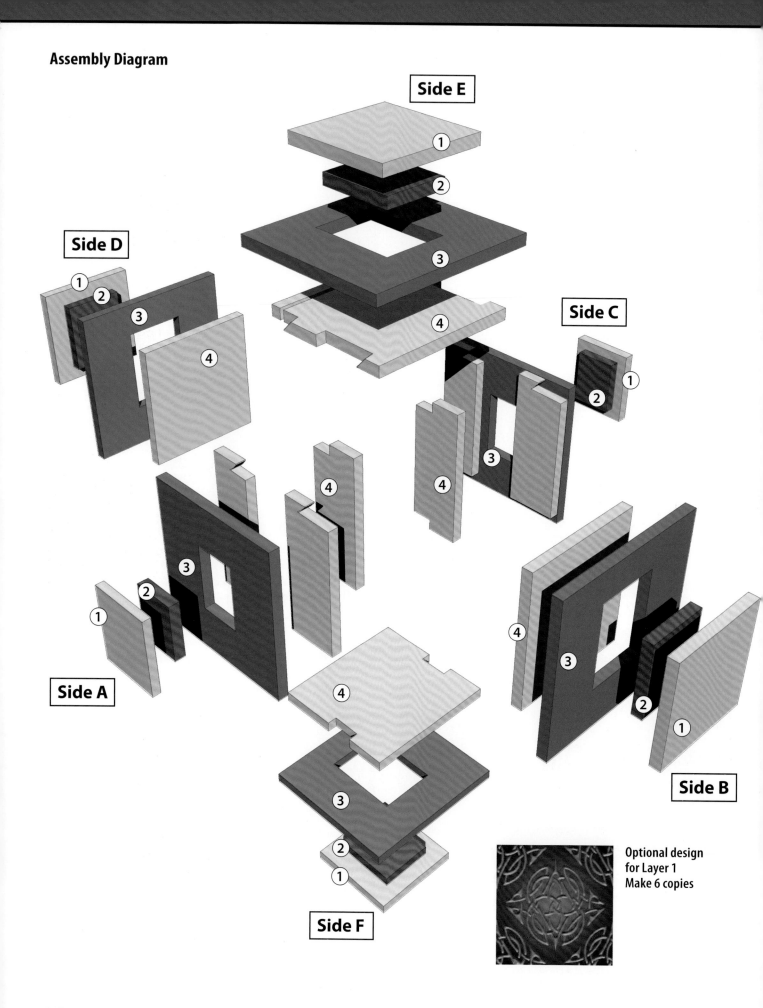

Side E

Side D

Side C

Side A

Side B

Side F

Optional design
for Layer 1
Make 6 copies

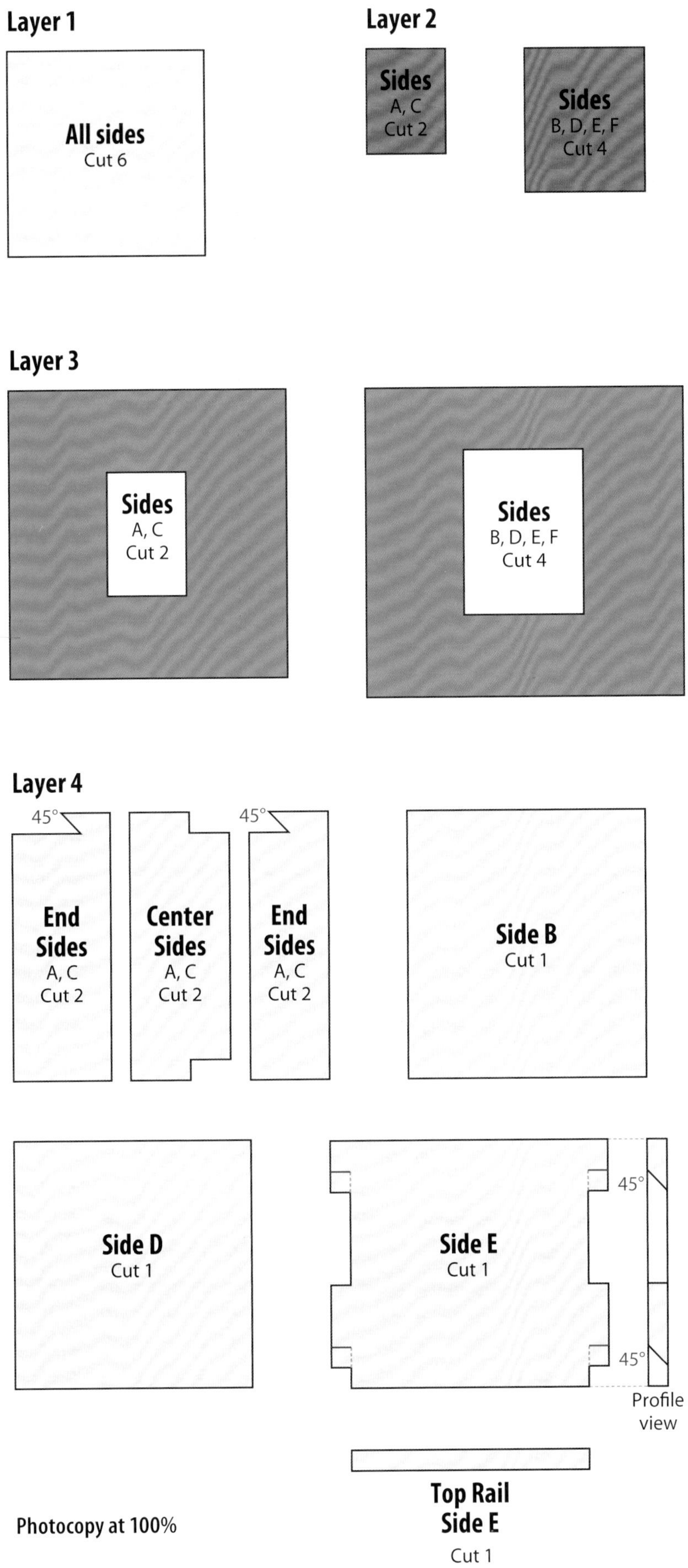

Layer 1

All sides
Cut 6

Layer 2

Sides
A, C
Cut 2

Sides
B, D, E, F
Cut 4

Layer 3

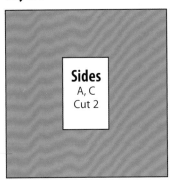

Sides
A, C
Cut 2

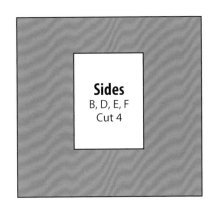

Sides
B, D, E, F
Cut 4

Layer 4

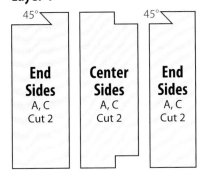

45°   45°

End Sides
A, C
Cut 2

Center Sides
A, C
Cut 2

End Sides
A, C
Cut 2

Side B
Cut 1

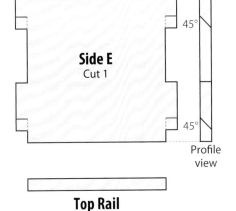

Side D
Cut 1

Side E
Cut 1

45°

45°

Profile view

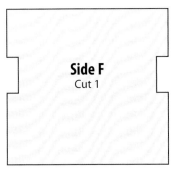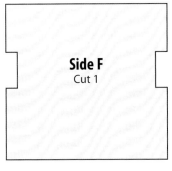

Side F
Cut 1

Top Rail Side E
Cut 1

Photocopy at 100%

Materials:

Make all panels from cherry or wood of choice
- 2 pieces ⅛" x 1¾" x 1¾" (layer 3, sides A and C)
- 4 pieces ⅛" x 1⅞" x 2" (layer 3, sides B, D, E, and F)
- 2 pieces ⅛" x ½" x ⅝" (layer 2, sides A and C)
- 4 pieces ⅛" x ¾" x ⅞" (layer 2, sides B, D, E, and F)
- ⅛" x 1⅝" x 1¾" (layer 4, side F)
- ⅛" x 1½" x 1¾" (layer 4, side E)
- ⅛" x 1½" x 1⅝" (layer 4, side B)
- ⅛" x 1½" x 1½" (layer 4, side D)
- 4 pieces ⅛" x ⅝" x 1⅝" (layer 4, end panels, sides A and C)
- 2 pieces ⅛" x ⅝" x 1⅝" (layer 4, center panel, sides A and C)
- 6 pieces ⅛" x 1¼" x 1¼" (layer 1, all sides)
- ⅛" x ⅛" x 1½" (top rail)
- Wood glue
- Assorted grits of sandpaper
- Light brown stain and varnish or finish of choice
- Artist fixative and printed design (optional)

Tools:

- #5 reverse-tooth blades or blades of choice
- Drill with ¹⁄₁₆"-diameter drill bit
- Assorted clamps
- Brushes to apply finish
- Bench knife
- Woodburner or carving tools (optional)

Secret Chamber Puzzle Box

Clever box with heart-shaped key is easy to make on your scroll saw

By Karl Taylor
Pine box cut by Ben Fink

During a band saw demonstration at our woodworking club, the instructor said certain projects could only be made with a band saw. Loving a good challenge, I proclaimed anything made on a band saw could also be made on a scroll saw—only smaller. For the next several months, club members proved my assertion by displaying their large projects along with a duplicate version made in miniature. That demonstration and the creativity of my fellow club members inspired this puzzle box. I adapted band saw techniques to meet the scroll saw's capabilities.

I make these puzzle boxes in a variety of sizes and shapes. Once you understand the technique, get creative. As long as the wood will fit your scroll saw, you can use it to make the box. I have made boxes as large as 1" by 1" by 12" and as small as ¼" by ¼" by 1". For smaller boxes, you need to use smaller blades.

Before you begin, use a small square to make sure your saw blade is exactly perpendicular to your table. This is critical for proper movement of the box parts. Check to make sure the blade is still square to the table throughout the process.

Remove the key and slide the lid off to reveal the secret chamber.

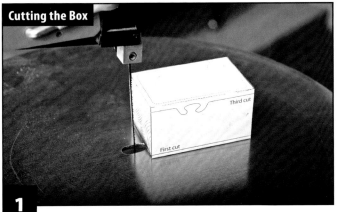

1 **Cut the box blank to the desired size and shape.** You can add round corners, a zigzag shape, or leave it square. Choose the most appealing side of blank for the top of the box. Place a piece of masking tape on the side, indicating the top and bottom.

2 **Cut the bottom of the box.** Fold the pattern on the dotted line and attach the pattern to the blank or make a mark ⅛" up from the bottom. Make sure your blade is square to the saw table and cut along the red line. Set the bottom aside for now.

3 **Cut the locking key out of the main section of the box.** Draw the key on with a pencil or use the pattern provided. I make keys shaped like hearts, stars, and T's. Cut the key and set it aside.

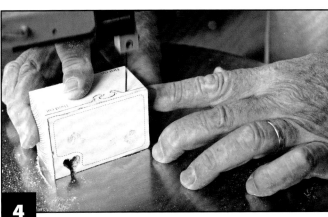

4 **Cut the box lid.** With the key removed from the main box, cut the sliding lid. Follow along the green line on the pattern or draw a similar line on the side of the box. Cut along the line with a #7 reverse-tooth blade. Slide the lid off and set it aside.

5 **Cut the chamber.** Draw a line ⅛" in from the edge the entire way around the blank. The line goes around the key slot, as shown with the dotted line on the pattern. Drill a small blade entry hole in one corner and cut along the line. Save both pieces.

6 **Cut the chamber lid.** Sketch a line about ⅛" below the top of the solid piece cut in Step 5. Ignore the puzzle lobe, but follow the general contour. Cut along this line with a #7 reverse-tooth blade. Set the top chamber lid piece (with the puzzle lobe) aside.

7 **Cut the risers.** Draw a line ⅛" in from both ends of the solid piece left over from Step 6. Cut along these lines. These end pieces will become risers that fit inside the chamber and support the chamber lid.

8 **Glue the box sides to the bottom.** Apply a small amount of glue along the bottom edge of the box sides. Do not apply any glue around the key slot area. Position the bottom panel on the box sides and remove any glue squeeze-out.

9 **Attach the risers.** Apply small amounts of glue to the inside ends of the box sides. Place the risers cut in Step 7 in position on both ends. Remove any glue squeeze-out above the risers. Replace the chamber lid to hold the risers in position.

10 **Finish assembling the box.** Carefully slide the top into place. Do not install the key. Use bar clamps to apply even pressure on the box bottom. Remove any glue squeeze-out and allow the glue to dry overnight.

11 **Sand the box.** Use a sanding block to sand away any remaining pencil marks. Sand the rough edges smooth.

12 **Apply a finish.** I use Danish oil followed by a coat of paste wax. A spray lacquer will also work. Finish all of the components.

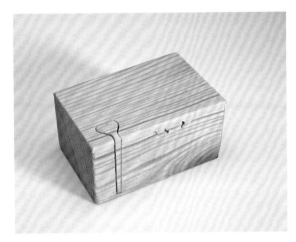

Puzzle Box Pattern

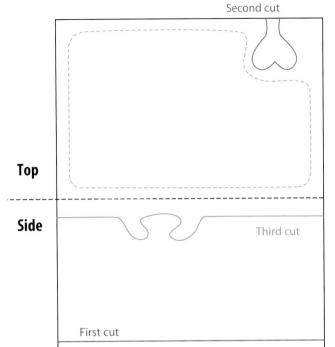

Second cut

Top

Alternative key design

© 2009 Scroll Saw Woodworking & Crafts

Side

Third cut

First cut

Photocopy at 100%

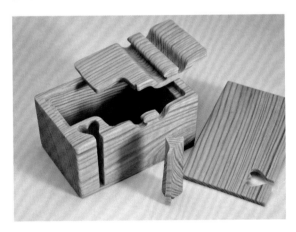

Experiment with different shapes for unique box styles.

Materials:
- 1⅝" x 1⅞" x 3" hardwood or wood of choice
- Tacky glue (white or clear)
- Danish oil and paste wax or finish of choice

Tools:
- #7 reverse-tooth blades or blades of choice
- Pencil with sharp point
- Ruler or other marking device
- Drill with comparable bit sized to scroll saw blade
- Small bar clamps
- Small square or 90° angle gauge
- 150-grit sanding block

TIPS DRAWING CUTTING LINES

- *Mark the wood lightly with a pencil*
- *If using a dark wood, try using a white pencil*

Slope-Sided Box

Create a charming, rustic-looking container from found wood

By Jim Stirling

You never know when and where you might find a piece of wood meant for your scroll saw. This box was created from a stout, dry oak limb.

This box is made using the principle of the sloping core cut. Tilting the table while cutting out the core will produce a conical piece that slips down snuggly into the case of the box. Slicing this core will then produce a base for the box and a lid-retaining ring. The principle can be used to make many other shapes of boxes. Examples of pieces I have made are a map of Australia and a maple leaf. A heart-shaped box is a winner for Valentine's Day.

Preparation

Cut a suitable section for the box off the branch with a handsaw. Then, slice it horizontally on the band saw. The first cut removes the bark and ¼" of material on one side to form the base of the box. Using this flat surface against the guide, then slice the material into two pieces, one forming the case of the box and the other the lid. Each piece must be thin enough to be able to pass under the arm of the scroll saw. In our case, each piece had to be less than 2" high.

Materials & Tools

Materials:
- Handsaw
- 1 piece, 2½" x 6" x 3" dry branch wood, with bark still on
- Pencil
- Sandpaper, 100 grit
- Wood glue

Tools:
- Band saw
- Drill with ¹⁄₁₆"-diameter bit
- Ruler
- #9 blades
- Belt sander

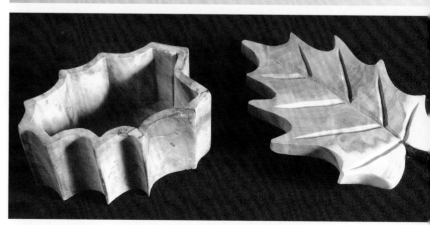

Boxes showing the shape of Australia and a maple leaf are other examples of scrolling using the sloping core cut principle.

Marking and Measuring

1 **Check the height.** Before starting, make sure the height of the wood fits under your saw's arm. The cutting height for each piece of this project should be no more than 2".

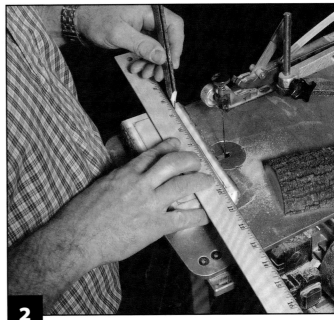

2 **Mark the inside area.** The piece that is flat on both sides will form the case of the box. Place this on the table with the widest side up. Using a pencil and ruler, mark straight lines about ¼" in from the bark on both sides. Also mark similar lines ¼" from the ends. Round off the corners to make a rectangle on the top of the piece.

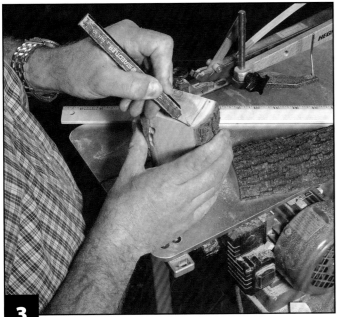

3 **Mark the sides.** Turn the same piece over and, using a pencil, make a straight line about ¼" from the bark on the two long sides. On the ends of the wood, mark lines that connect the longitudinal lines on the top to the bottom longitudinal lines. These lines will be used to indicate the amount of table tilt when cutting.

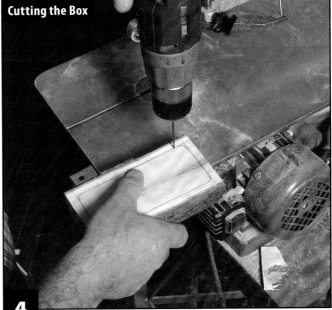

Cutting the Box

4 **Drill a blade entry hole.** Place the wood on the saw table in front of the blade. Using the back left hand mark as a guide, push down the right hand side of the table until the blade is parallel with this line. Leave the block of wood where it is on the table, and using a hand drill and a ¹⁄₁₆"-diameter bit, make a blade entry hole somewhere along the left longitudinal line. You should be able to bore vertically. If the drill is too short to go all the way through the wood, make a drill bit from wire. Cut wire that is about the same diameter of the bit and about 3" to 4" long. Sharpen the end on the belt sander into a chisel shape and put it into the drill chuck. You should be able to drill the remainder of the hole with this. Don't drill into the scroll saw table.

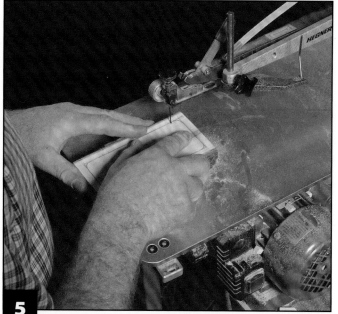

5 **Insert a #9 blade into the blade entry hole and install the blade in place.** Cut out the rectangular core in a counterclockwise direction. Remember to be patient with your cutting. With this thickness of wood, the blade is really being put to the test. Too much pressure will break the blade; too little will overheat it.

6 **Remove the conical core from the box case and then remove the blade from the center of the case.**

Marking the Base

7 **Mark the base.** Push the core piece into the case until it stops, and using a pencil, draw a line around the bottom of the case onto the protruding base. There was about ⅟₁₆" protruding on my box, but your results may vary, depending on the angle of the cut.

8 **Mark the base ring and cut the core.** Remove the core piece. Mark off the base of the box. Using the pencil and your curled middle finger as a guide, make a rectangular mark ¼" above the mark you made in the last step. Next, mark off the lid-retaining ring. Draw a similar rectangular line ¼" down from the topside of the core. If the core is small enough, slice it on the scroll saw; otherwise use a band saw. The table will still be tilted at the proper angle, so that when the core is placed on its side, the blade will cut vertical slices through the wood. Cut along all three marks. This will produce four slices of wood. Only the top and third from top pieces will be used.

9 **Cut the lid-retaining ring.** Take the top slice, and using your pencil and third finger as a guide, mark off a rectangle about ¼" from the edges. Drill a blade entry hole and cut out the core as done in Step 5.

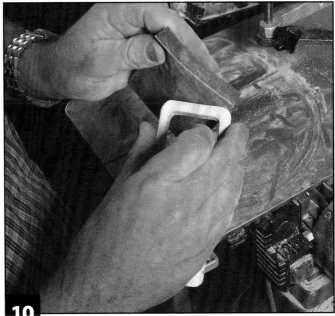

10 **Sand the lid-retaining ring.** The lid-retaining ring will be glued onto the bottom of the lid to hold the lid in place. This lid ring will fit snugly into the top of the box. Using 100-grit sandpaper, gently sand this piece smooth. Also, sand the bottom of the lid.

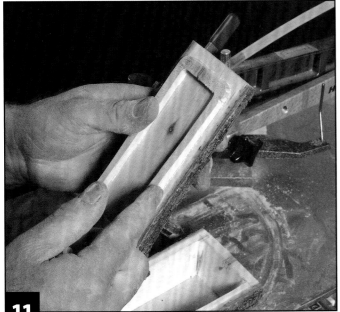

11 **Attach the ring.** Follow these instructions to help correctly position the lid-retaining ring: Place the lid upside down, and place the box case upside down on top of this. Align the edges of both pieces. Then, take your pencil and mark around where the inner edge of the case meets the underside of the lid. Using wood glue, glue the retaining ring onto the bottom of the lid. To ensure a good bond, apply some pressure. Put the lid and ring down on a flat surface, and then balance something weighing a couple of pounds on top. Allow the glue to dry for a couple of hours.

Finishing

12 **Attach the bottom and sand.** Using the belt sander, smooth the ¼"-thick rectangle piece, which will be inserted into the box and become the bottom. Glue the bottom into the box. Push the bottom out until it fits snugly. After the glue is dry, you may need to use the belt sander to sand the bottom of the box.

Mirrored Flower Box with Copper and Patina

A versatile weekend project

By Donna and Phil Racine

Making this mirrored box is a relatively straightforward process. In fact, you should have no trouble creating it in a weekend or less. The fun part is the finish. The simulated patina and copper add a handsome touch to the mirror and box. We chose to put silk flowers in the box, but it also makes a nice catchall for watches, pins, and clips that tend to collect on your bureau.

Step 1: Prepare the wood. Sand and wipe off the dust so it will accept the patterns.

Step 2: Make copies of the pattern and save the original. Take the photocopies of the Back, Top, and Box (left, right, front) patterns and spray them with temporary bond adhesive. Attach the patterns to the wood.

Step 3: Drill blade entry holes in the Top. Use the ⅛"-diameter bit. Thread the #2/0 through a hole and cut it out as indicated on the pattern. Repeat threading and cutting until all of the holes are cut out. Use the 120-grit sandpaper to remove burrs.

Step 4: Assemble the box. Put the box together in this order: Front, sides, and bottom. Glue and nail with ⅜" brads as indicated. Do NOT attach the back at this time.

Step 5: Patina the wood. Work according to directions in the kit, or finish the individual parts to suit. The patina can be a little messy, so use rubber gloves.

Step 6: Attach the box to the back. Use Copper Pattern #1 and fold it along the lines indicated. Insert it into the box and use the epoxy to spot glue the copper into the box. The copper ends run between the back and the inside of the box, which secures the copper. Finish by gluing the bottom and nailing the side with either the ⅜" or the ½" brads.

Step 7: Add the copper circles. Using scissors, cut twelve ¾" circles using Copper Pattern #3. Attach the copper circles to the back of the front using epoxy. Make sure the glue stays on the edges and does not run into the center of the copper circle. Center and align the top as desired. Attach the top to the back using ⅜" brads and glue.

Step 8: Cut Copper Pattern #2. Attach it to the back using glue, brads, or tape.

Step 9: Insert the mirror and cardboard backing. Secure them into the sides with ½" brads. If you wish to hang the mirror flower box, simply add a hanger.

Right Side Lid

Left Side Lid

Cut two copies of this pattern. The blue markings are for the left side; the red markings are for the right side.

Left Side

Right Side

Box Front

Photocopy at 100%

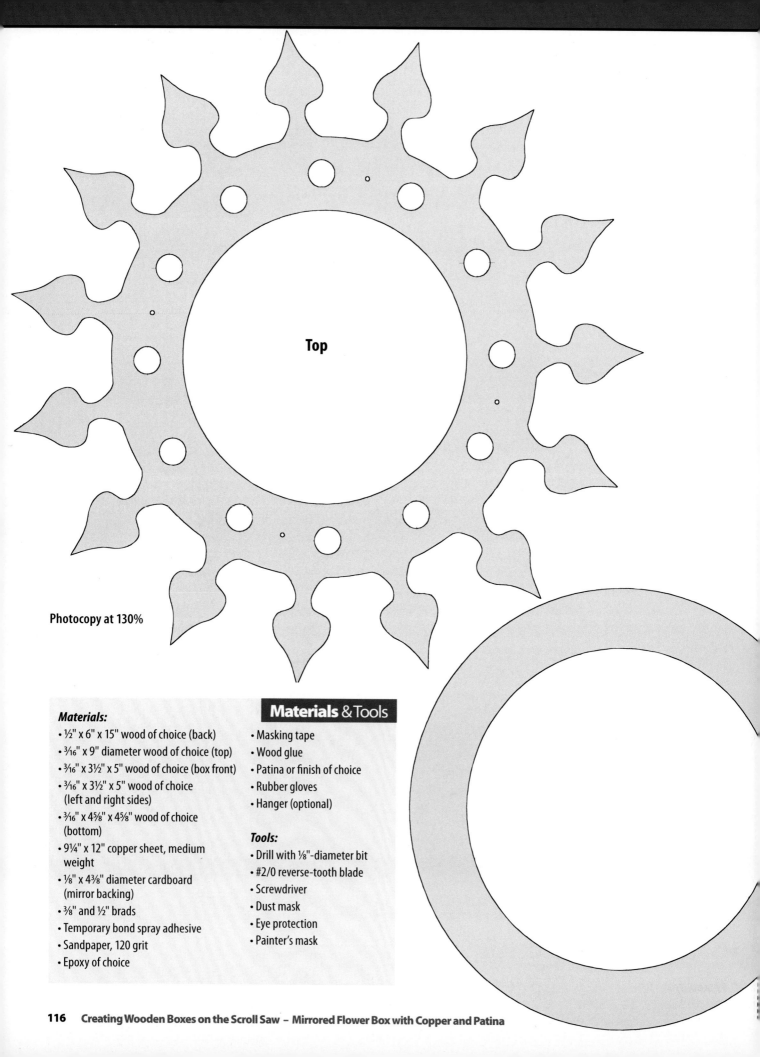

Top

Photocopy at 130%

Materials:

- ½" x 6" x 15" wood of choice (back)
- ³⁄₁₆" x 9" diameter wood of choice (top)
- ³⁄₁₆" x 3½" x 5" wood of choice (box front)
- ³⁄₁₆" x 3½" x 5" wood of choice (left and right sides)
- ³⁄₁₆" x 4⅝" x 4⅝" wood of choice (bottom)
- 9¼" x 12" copper sheet, medium weight
- ⅛" x 4⅜" diameter cardboard (mirror backing)
- ⅜" and ½" brads
- Temporary bond spray adhesive
- Sandpaper, 120 grit
- Epoxy of choice

Materials & Tools

- Masking tape
- Wood glue
- Patina or finish of choice
- Rubber gloves
- Hanger (optional)

Tools:

- Drill with ⅛"-diameter bit
- #2/0 reverse-tooth blade
- Screwdriver
- Dust mask
- Eye protection
- Painter's mask

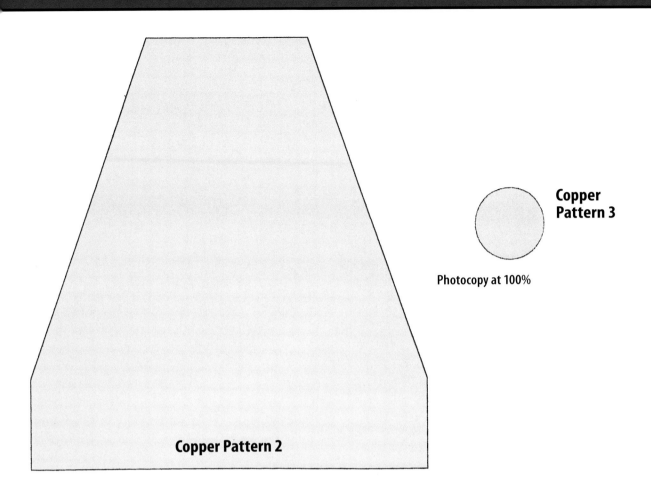

Copper Pattern 3

Photocopy at 100%

Copper Pattern 2

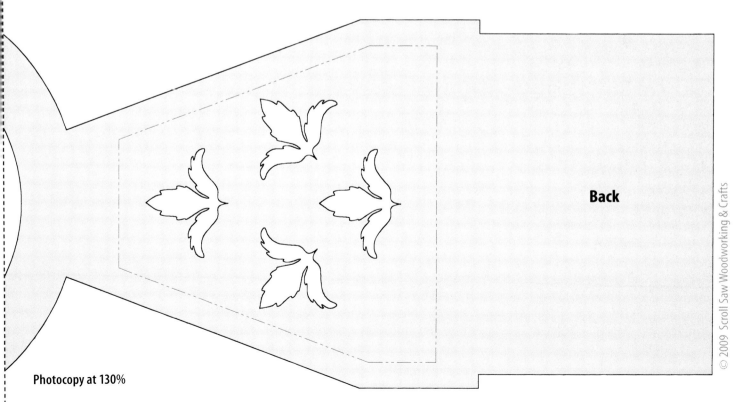

Back

Photocopy at 130%

Magazine Storage Case

Easy-to-make cases solve your magazine and pattern storage problems

By Dennis Simmons

If you're like me, there's a pile of back issues of *Scroll Saw Workshop/Scroll Saw Woodworking & Crafts* next to your favorite chair—the rest are gathering dust on the corner of the workbench.

The management of our home (my lovely wife) suggested I get them organized, so this project is my solution. These magazine storage cases keep the magazines neat and clean and look nice on the family book shelf.

The storage case is a simple box that is open in the back. The design includes an optional divider panel so pattern insert sections can be stored along with the magazines.

Begin the project by cutting all of the pieces to the dimensions listed on the materials list. I use a piece of poplar for the decorative front and pine and plywood for the remaining pieces. Mark a centerline on the pattern and the blank to make it easy to align the two properly. Transfer the pattern to the blank, using your method of choice.

Note: Not all ¼"-thick plywood is a full ¼" thick. Most commercial plywood is actually 5mm thick, which is closer to ³⁄₁₆". The patterns and dimensions listed here are for 5mm-thick plywood. If you use true ¼"-thick plywood, you may need to adjust the dimensions accordingly.

Materials & Tools

Materials:
- ¼" x 4" x 12" poplar (letter board)
- ⅜" x 3½" x 11¼" pine (backing board)
- 2 pieces ⅜" x 3⅝" x 9¼" pine (top and bottom)
- ¼" x 8⅞" x 12" plywood (divider panel)
- 2 pieces ¼" x 9¼" x 12" plywood (side panels)
- Glue stick, temporary bond spray adhesive, or transfer paper (to transfer pattern to blanks)
- Wood glue
- Cyanoacrylate gel glue
- 18 brads (small nails)
- Sandpaper, 150 grit
- Polyurethane varnish

Tools:
- #0 skip-tooth blades or blades of choice
- Drill with ¹⁄₁₆"-diameter twist bit

Cutting the Case

1 **Cut the letters using a #0 skip-tooth blade.** Drill the blade entry holes using a ¹⁄₁₆"-diameter twist bit and remove any burrs. Cut the centers from letters such as *a*, *p*, and *o* first and set them aside to be glued back in later. Sand off burrs on the back after cutting each letter.

2 **Glue the letter board to the backing board.** The backing board wood color should contrast with the decorative front. Mark guidelines ⅜" from the edges on the back of the decorative front and apply wood glue inside the guidelines. Clamp the backing board in place until dry. Attach the centers cut from the open letters with a few drops of cyanoacrylate glue. Hold the pieces in place with tweezers for 15 to 20 seconds while the glue dries.

3 **Cut the notches and mortises for the divider panel.** Use the scroll saw to cut notches in the divider panel and rectangular mortise holes in the top and bottom pieces as shown on the pattern.

Assembling and Finishing the Case

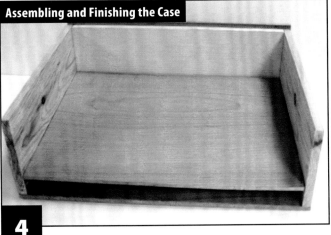

4 **Assemble the storage case.** Apply a little wood glue on the edges to be joined and secure with a few brads while the glue dries. Attach the top to the backing board, insert the notches of the divider panel into the mortises, and attach the bottom to the backing board.

5 **Finish the cases.** Attach the side panels with glue and brads and allow them to dry. Sand all of the surfaces with 150-grit sandpaper. Then, finish the project with three coats of thinned polyurethane varnish or your finish of choice.

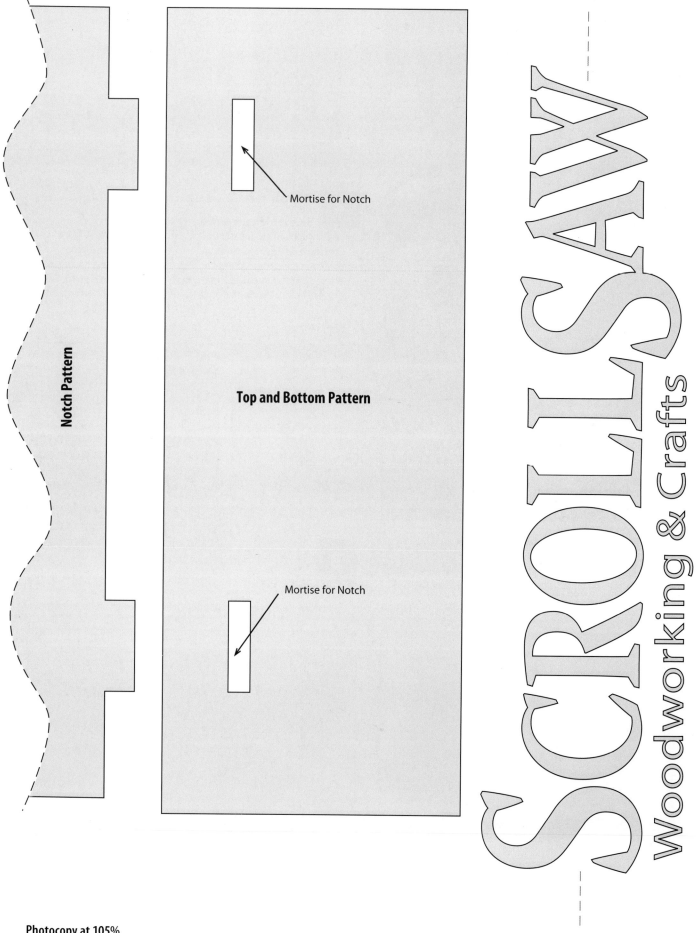

Notch Pattern

Mortise for Notch

Top and Bottom Pattern

Mortise for Notch

SCROLL SAW

Woodworking & Crafts

© 2009 Scroll Saw Woodworking & Crafts

Photocopy at 105%

Ribbons and Bows Box

Easy compound-cut bow adds elegance to this custom gift box

By Carole Rothman

Decked out with ribbons and bows, this stunning box adds a personal touch to the presentation of a special gift. It can also be used as a jewelry or trinket box or as a candy dish.

I combined my knowledge of scrolling with my experience making sugar paste bows for cakes. The result is a gift box with a bow that looks so real, people touch it to be sure it's really made of wood.

The project consists of two parts: a lidded box embellished with a ribbon, and a compound-cut bow. Careful alignment of the parts and thorough sanding are the keys to a beautiful project.

You can use a solid color wood for the ribbons, but the laminated blanks used to create the striped effect add to the charm of this project. The blanks are made from cherry and purpleheart glued together in an alternating pattern. To create the blanks for the flat ribbons and the tails, glue and clamp two ¼"-thick strips of purpleheart on either side of a ¼"-thick strip of cherry. The blank for the ribbon loops is made the same way, but additional ⅛"-thick strips of cherry are glued on the outside edges to get the full 1" width (see the materials list for full dimensions).

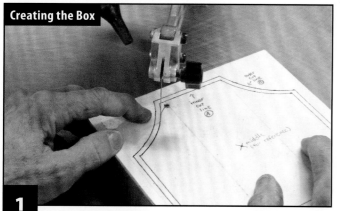

1 **Cut the inside of the box.** Attach the pattern to the wood with spray adhesive and cover the pattern with clear packaging tape. Drill a ⅛"-diameter blade entry hole inside the box and cut along the inner line with a #9 reverse-tooth blade. Remove the fuzzies on the bottom with sandpaper. Sand the sides smooth. Do not remove the pattern.

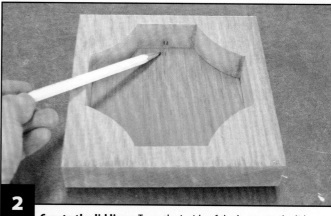

2 **Create the lid liner.** Trace the inside of the box onto the lid liner stock. Make a small pencil mark on the inside of the box and on the liner stock for easier alignment. Cut along the traced line with a #3 reverse-tooth blade. Sand the edges smooth so the liner fits just inside the box. The liner keeps the lid aligned properly so the ribbons look realistic.

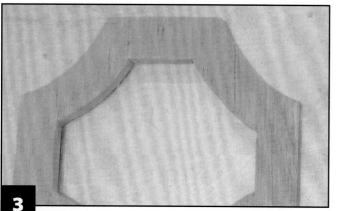

3 **Cut the center of the lid liner.** This will prevent the lid from warping. Draw a line ¾" in from the outside edge of the lid liner. Drill a blade entry hole and cut out the center of the lid liner. Sand the lid liner smooth.

TIPS

SHARP INSIDE CORNERS
Cutting a clean corner with a large blade and thick wood is a four-step process. Cut to each corner, back off, then cut a gentle curve to the next side. Go back and cut into the corner from the other direction after the interior waste has been removed.

REDUCE YOUR CUTTING
Use the blade entry hole to form the inside curve of the ribbon loop. This reduces the need to make sharp turns in the thick, laminated stock.

PRECISE GLUING
Use a glue syringe so you can put the glue exactly where you want it when gluing the loops and tails. I use glue that sets up quickly and dries clear.

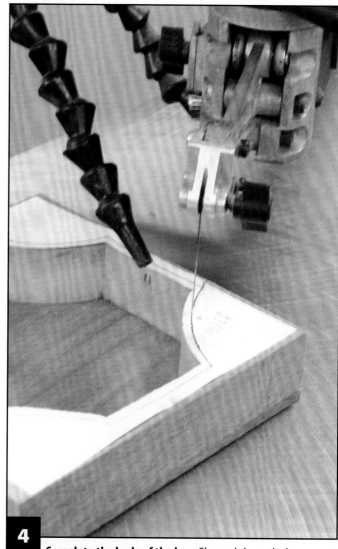

4 **Complete the body of the box.** Glue and clamp the box sides to the box bottom stock. Align the grain of the box sides and the box bottom. Cut along the outer line of the box with a #12 reverse-tooth blade. Sand the outside of the box smooth.

5 **Cut the lid.** Trace the outside of the box on the lid stock. Align the grain of the box with the lid. Make a pencil mark on the lid and a corresponding mark on the box so you can realign them later. Cut along the outside of the lid with a #3 reverse-tooth blade. Realign the lid and box, and attach the lid to the box with masking tape. Sand the sides of the lid flush with the box sides.

6 **Glue the lid liner to the lid.** Center the liner on the lid. Invert the box on the lid and align the marks made earlier. Adjust the box until the edges are flush. Lift the box carefully, leaving the liner in position. Trace around the liner with a pencil. Align the liner on the line, and glue and clamp it in place. Let the glue dry, and sand both using progressively finer sandpaper up to 320 grit.

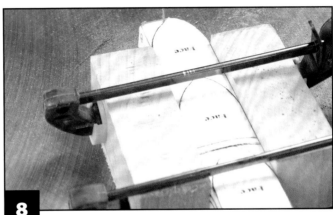

Cutting the Ribbons and Bows

7 **Cut the open loops.** Fold the six loop patterns along the dotted line and attach them to the laminated blank, aligning the fold with the corner of the blank. Drill blade entry holes at the curve of the loop with a ⅜"-diameter brad-point bit. Cut the insides and the outsides of the loops, starting at the bottom, with a #12 blade. Remove the waste, but leave the loop in place.

8 **Cut the sides of the loops.** Rotate the blank. Place small wood blocks just above the ends of the curved cutting lines on the first loop. Clamp the blocks together to hold the loop in place while you cut. Cut along each side, starting at the bottom point. Loosen the clamps and remove the loop. Cut along the top line of the loop face to clear the waste. Cut and sand the remaining loops.

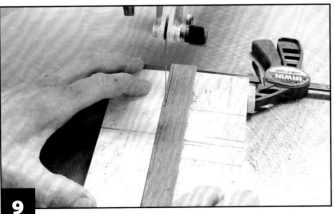

9 **Cut the flat ribbons.** Use scrap wood to clamp the stock for easier handling. Cut a ¹⁄₁₆"-thick strip from the laminated stock and sand the blank smooth. Cut three more strips using the same process. Sand each strip smooth. If you are not comfortable sanding the strips, wait until you glue them in place in Step 11.

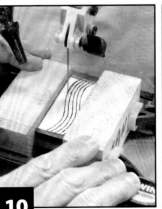

10 **Cut the tails.** Attach the tails pattern to the laminated blank. Cut the sides of the tails using support blocks and clamps. Tape the tails and waste back together with clear tape, secure with scrap blocks and clamps, and cut the face of the tails. Sand the pieces smooth and taper the edges for a realistic look.

11 Attach the flat top ribbons. Mark the center of each flat side on the lid and box. Cut a flat ribbon ⅛" longer than the width of the lid, with a 45° angle on each end. Position the ribbon on the centerline and measure from the ribbon to the box edge on the other centerline. Cut two more strips, each ¹⁄₁₆" longer than this measurement, with a 45° angle on one end. Glue the ribbons on the lines, angled-side down. The ribbons hang ¹⁄₁₆" over the edges.

12 Attach the four side ribbons. Cut the side ribbons about 1" longer than the height of the box and lid. Cut one end of each at a 45° angle. Position the angled end against the angled end of the top ribbon. Mark the bottom of the lid and the bottom of the box. Cut each ribbon on the lines and glue the pieces to the lid and the box side. After the glue dries, place the lid on the box and sand the ribbons smooth. Round the top and bottom edges of the ribbons.

13 Attach the tails to the lid. Dry fit the tails on the lid and adjust the length and fit of the pointed end with sandpaper. Apply glue to the pointed ends and position them on the lid. Prop the ends up with blocks of foam or wood until the glue dries. Dry fit five loops in a ring around the intersection of the top ribbons. Sand the sides of the loops to make them fit tightly together.

14 Attach the loops. Glue the loops in place. Sand the point of the remaining center loop to shorten and flatten it. Glue it in place in the center of the ring of loops. Carefully rub the entire box down with #0000 steel wool to remove any remaining fuzz or scratches. Then, apply several coats of spray shellac or your finish of choice. A spray finish is easiest to apply because of the ribbons.

Variations

Use the same lamination series for the loops and ribbons or use a solid color for both. You can cut the flat ribbons very thin and use a butt joint where the top meets the sides of the box instead of a miter joint.

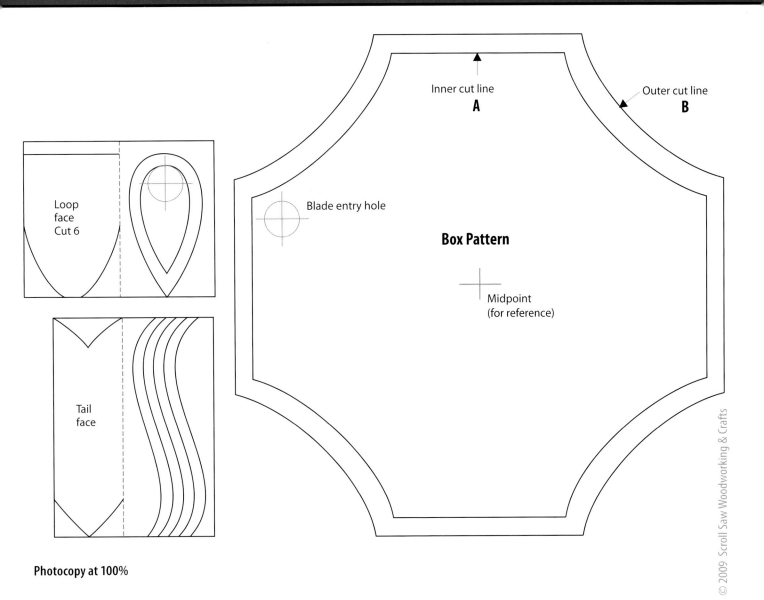

Loop face
Cut 6

Tail face

Inner cut line
A

Outer cut line
B

Blade entry hole

Box Pattern

Midpoint
(for reference)

© 2009 Scroll Saw Woodworking & Crafts

Photocopy at 100%

Materials:
- Temporary bond spray adhesive
- Wood glue (I use Weldbond)
- Plastic glue syringe (precise glue placement)
- Clear packing tape
- Assorted grits of sandpaper up to 320 grit
- Spray shellac (gloss) or finish of choice
- #0000 steel wool

BOX:
- ¾" to 1¼" x 6" x 6" mahogany or walnut (box sides)
- 2 pieces ¼" x 6" x 6" mahogany or walnut (bottom and lid)
- ¼" x 5½" x 5½" Baltic birch plywood or wood of choice (lid liner)

LOOPS: 1" x 1" x 10½" laminated blank made up of strips of:
- ¼"-thick cherry
- 2 pieces ¼"-thick purpleheart
- 2 pieces ⅛"-thick cherry

RIBBONS: ¾" x 1" x 6" laminated blank made up of strips of:
- ¼"-thick cherry
- 2 pieces ¼"-thick purpleheart

TAILS: ¾" x 1" x 2½" laminated blank made up of strips of:
- ¼"-thick cherry
- 2 pieces ¼"-thick purpleheart

Materials & Tools

Tools:
- #3, #9, and #12 reverse-tooth blades or blades of choice
- Drill
- ⅛"-diameter drill bit
- ⅜"-diameter brad-point drill bit
- Vertical and spindle sanders or sanding blocks
- Support blocks (clamping)
- 2 clamps, 6" (compound cutting, thin ribbons)
- Clamps for gluing box and lid
- Scraps of foam or wood (to support tails while glue dries)

Contributors

Robert Ardizzoni
Robert lives in Holland, Mass., and designs projects for his six children and 14 grandchildren.

Kenneth Campbell
Ken lives in Delano, Calif., and won *SSWC*'s Best Project Design Contest.

Sue Chrestensen
Sue enjoys spending her time designing and pursuing her love for scroll sawing and is the founder of the MSN group for Scrollsaw Crafters.
www.chrestensenburghoutdesigns.com

Rick and Karen Longabaugh
Rick and Karen own The Berry Basket and Great American Scrollsaw Patterns.
www.greatamericanscrollsaw.com

Gary MacKay
Gary lives in Myrtle Beach, S.C., and enjoys gardening and golf.

Paul Meisel
Paul resides in Mound, Minn., where he is an avid woodworker and designer.

Sue Mey
Sue lives in Pretoria, South Africa.
www.scrollsawartist.com

John A. Nelson
John, a prolific scroller and designer, contributes frequently to *Scroll Saw Woodworking & Crafts*.
www.scrollsawer.com

Joe Preston
Joe lives in Nassau, N.Y., with his wife, Lianne, and runs a part-time business called Jo-Li Creations.

Donna and Phil Racine
Donna and Phil live in Ascutney, Vt., and operate P & D Woodworking and Design from their home.
www.scrollsawpatterncenter.com

Carole Rothman
Carole, of Somers, N.Y., is a retired psychologist and college professor and is also an award-winning cake decorator.

Dennis Simmons
Dennis, author of *Making Furniture and Dollhouses for American Girl and Other 18-Inch Dolls*, lives in Rushville, Ind.,
Intarsiawood@hotmail.com

Jim Stirling
Australian-born Jim is known for using his unique relief techniques to scroll collapsible castles. He lives in Norway.
www.stirling.no

Karl Taylor
Karl is a self-taught scroller and an active instructor from Lawrenceville, Ga., who gives demonstrations for DeWalt, PS Woods, and Dremel.

Diana Thompson
Diana, who lives in Theodore, Ala., is a prolific scroller and designer.
www.scrollsawinspirations.com

Dave Van Ess
Dave, of Arlington, Wash., started woodworking more than 30 years ago and has taught classes in scroll sawing.

Bruce Viney
Bruce, of Washington, England, enjoys designing and making puzzles and puzzle boxes.
www.homemadepuzzles.co.uk

Joan West
Joan makes her home in Cedar Rapids, Iowa, and loves making functional projects in wood.

Index

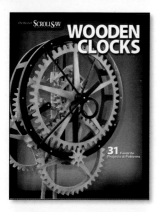
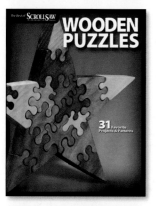

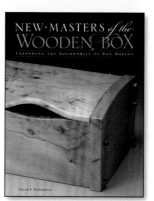
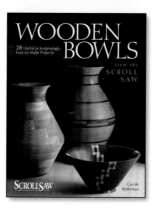